MANAGING
WHEN TIMES ARE
TOUGH

MANAGING
WHEN TIMES ARE
TOUGH

THEO J. VAN DIJK

PRAEGER

AN IMPRINT OF ABC-CLIO, LLC
Santa Barbara, California • Denver, Colorado • Oxford, England

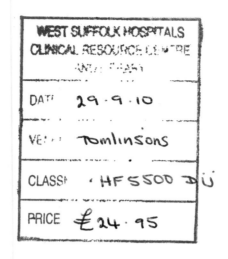
Library of Congress Cataloging-in-Publication Data

Dijk, Theo J. van
    Managing when times are tough / Theo J. van Dijk.
        p. cm.
    Includes bibliographical references and index.
    ISBN 978-0-313-38159-1 (alk. paper) — ISBN 978-0-313-38160-7 (e-book)
1. Industrial management. 2. Business ethics. I. Title.
    HD31.D533 2010
    658—dc22   2009048774

ISBN: 978-0-313-38159-1
EISBN: 978-0-313-38160-7

14 13 12 11 10   1 2 3 4 5

This book is also available on the World Wide Web as an eBook.
Visit www.abc-clio.com for details.

Praeger
An Imprint of ABC-CLIO, LLC

ABC-CLIO, LLC
130 Cremona Drive, P.O. Box 1911
Santa Barbara, California 93116-1911

This book is printed on acid-free paper ∞
Manufactured in the United States of America

To my grandson
Domenico
Not yet 3, he stands at the very beginning
of his own personal journey.

Contents

Acknowledgments

A management book written by a seasoned international interim general manager can be anchored only in all the experiences from the various businesses, cultural environments, and employees encountered. In particular, the writer wishes to express his thanks to the many managers, young and old, who comprised "his" management teams over the years in many businesses and in quite a few countries during mostly very challenging and often trying times.

Ken Wright of Wright Consultancy, Dublin, Ireland, a gifted team-development expert and motivator supreme, found time in his very busy schedule of international assignments for public and private enterprises in emerging economies to read the pre-edited manuscript and give me his comments. His insights never cease to amaze me.

David Wright, also of Wright Consultancy, Dublin, Ireland, an expert in developing work teams and motivator par excellence, gave freely of his time, read the pre-edited text and made some valuable suggestions. His sharp intellect gave me food for thought on many an occasion. Both David and Ken have been of great influence on what, for better or worse, are my own team- and employee-development skills.

Ian Stewart, Director of Genesys Systems Ltd., Dublin, Ireland, read the pre-edited text and gave me his thoughts on the material. His eminently practical approach to systems development and implementation for small and medium-sized enterprises (SMEs) is a breath of fresh air on a sea of mediocrity.

My oldest daughter, Judith, an Internet and Web design marketing professional, had some pretty useful comments on the marketing and sales topics in the pre-edited text and gave me frank feedback. My youngest daughter, Nicole, a sales executive for an international pharmaceutical company, made many remarks and observations on the pre-edited text and gave me her honest and sound opinion. It still gratifies me that both of them have done so well in their respective careers. I am indeed a very proud father.

My wife, Bridget, is my "first filter" and strength. If only she knew that my heart beat faster when she approved of a chapter but missed a couple of beats when she disapproved and rewriting was suggested. Her eye for detail is striking, and her family team management skills are phenomenal.

Without Jeff Olson, senior acquisition editor, business and economics, for Praeger Publishers this book would never have seen the light of day. Jeff really got me going once the topic was established from some material that I sent him a while back. His encouragements, remarks, and sound suggestions have made this book what it is; for his confidence in me and his expert guidance I am truly thankful.

To my Heavenly Father and Constant Inspirer goes my eternal gratitude. He encourages me, walks with me, and guides me in all that I do. As an often recalcitrant subject, I am amazed at the many blessings He has bestowed on me regardless.

CHAPTER 1

LET'S CRY A LITTLE, KICK THE FAT CAT, AND GET ON WITH IT

We have always known that heedless self-interest was bad morals: we know now that it is bad economics.

—Franklin D. Roosevelt (1882–1945)

WHAT GOT US ALL INTO THIS MESS OR, LET'S CRY A LITTLE

It's no secret anymore! The world economy (2009) is in its most terrifying state since the depression of the 1930s. Demand is slumping across the world. Businesses and consumers are confronted with dysfunctional financial markets, fast-disappearing wealth, pretty horrific unemployment, and widespread fear. The golden age of financial wizardry has been terminated abruptly, maybe for good, but for the time being anyway. We also have some pretty obnoxious scapegoats, but, let's be honest, we all share part of the blame. We came to believe that debt, including personal debt, didn't matter anymore and that somehow, sometime in the future it would all come out in the wash of fast-rising property values, increased wages, and so forth. Financial globalization spread capital far and wide, new markets developed, companies could readily finance new ventures, and just about every individual had unparalleled access to borrowing money at cheap rates. All these transactions were based on trust, the very essence of our financial system. In an interview with Edward Carr, Business Affairs Editor of the *Economist,* the *Economist* (2009) wrote,

> Trust's slow accumulation pushes financial markets forward; its shattering betrayal batters them back. Sometimes this is through bad faith, as when Bernie Madoff, a grand fund manager, allegedly made his investors $50 billion poorer, or mortgage-sellers tempted naïve borrowers. But promises made in good faith can be broken too. Indeed,

honest failure is even more corrosive of trust than outright criminality. Everyone understands that now.[1]

However, the lack of trust is not the only factor that has played a major part in the current financial crises. In boom times institutions that play it too safe cease to exist or are often gobbled up by others. Mediocrity doesn't appeal to boom markets. The successful and increasingly larger survivors are expected to go for ever greater returns, regardless of risk. This behavior is certainly driven on by the continuous scrutiny of packs of analysts, the frenzied hype of the media, and the short-term expectations of shareholders. In particular, the financial institutions were driven to ever greater risks with newly designed products.[2] If they didn't jump on the latest product bandwagon, but their competitors did, the market would punish them accordingly. So it became progressively more difficult to jump off the ever more quickly accelerating merry-go-round. Investment banks got bolder and bolder, and traditional banks felt that they had to get a part of the action too. A culture of universal greed prevailed at the management top of these financial institutions, as it did at some other corporations, I might add. Reward structures eventually, and certainly for sinking corporate ships, were shown to be devoid of any norms or sense of reality.

Property Booms and National Busts

In countries that saw massive property booms, an additional problem was created in the form of negative equity when the party was finally over. Home owners with quite substantial negative equity tend to minimize their spending habits, regardless of how well the banks are recapitalized. Without spending, the recession deepens, industry feels the effects of reduced spending, unemployment increases, tax revenues decrease, and so the negative cycle feeds on itself.

The well-known saying, "countries do not go bankrupt," is also being tested to the full by Iceland and other potential candidates, such as Ireland and Latvia. So there has been a scramble by quite a few countries to sell government bonds to finance massive deficits. These deficits were created almost overnight by bailing out the imploding banking sector with vast sums of taxpayers' money. The total rescue costs of this bailout are massive. The IMF predicts that average government debt in the richer G20 countries will exceed 100% of GDP by 2014, up from 70% in 2000.[3]

Buying government bonds on the open market is becoming riskier as well. This is reflected in the premium that some countries have to pay to investors on their long-term debt issues. Such countries now face a potential vicious circle: considerably higher financing costs weigh on economic activity, increasing both the size of the deficit and the cost of financing it. The accepted drastic remedy, to devalue the national currency, is no longer an option for countries in the Euro Zone.[4]

Overcapacity Problems and Government Involvement

A different problem that already existed for some time, but that was somehow never really taken too seriously, was overproduction in a number of industries. The steel, petrochemical, semiconductor, and car industries have been mentioned in this context. The latter is no doubt a stark example to which most of us can relate well. Already in 1987 it was noted that worldwide overcapacity in the car industry was between 15 and 20%.[5] A recent report in *Business Week* magazine puts this figure at a staggering 74%![6] Nevertheless, the knee-jerk response of governments in the United States, the United Kingdom, and France has been to support their local car industries. Some will say this is due to the fact that this industry is uncomfortably close to the consumer financial system, thereby possibly prolonging the agony of an inevitable scaleback, even if demand picks up again.

The one consequence of all this bad news is that, whether we like it or not, governments have become seriously involved in the financial services sector and, to a lesser extent, in the car industry. It's almost a central planning scenario like the one we so detested of late in Communist-run countries! Also, isn't it ironic that the same financiers who kept on preaching the necessity of free markets on the way up have since depended exclusively on taxpayers to save their industry at a cost of trillions of dollars?

Cash Is King Again

Another interesting consequence of this worldwide crisis has been the sudden change in attitude to that commodity we refer to as cash. Not more than a year ago (2008), to accumulate it was considered wasteful and even dangerous. Boards of Directors were urged to return cash to investors by means of special dividends or to buy back shares. Companies had to be as lean as possible, by outsourcing just about everything excluding core competencies, by getting heavily involved in just-in-time-supplier systems, and by loading up on debt to leverage the balance sheet. Organizations that hoarded cash, even ones as good as Toyota and Microsoft, were viewed with suspicion.[7] Now, barely a year later (2009), everyone knows what is meant by "monthly burn rate," and managers are urged to scoop up whatever cash they can find and then stash it for as long as possible! Against this background it's not surprising that a lot of companies were caught out when boom finally turned to bust.

Whom Can We Blame?

The main players in this still far from completed drama (2009) must surely be the top managers of financial institutions, financial regulators worldwide, and our respective politicians. The first group in particular rode the crest of the wave and got paid scandalous amounts of money. With the first weak signs of recovery recorded in the fall of 2009, some financial institutions should perhaps reconsider their business models and ask themselves the question, do we run a business for our employees or for our shareholders and customers?[8]

In many countries financial regulators lost the plot altogether. Whether this was due to their limited resources, their limited understanding, or their reliance on the "integrity" of even now far-too-powerful financial moguls will no doubt be debated for some time to come. One thing is for certain: regulators had better start doing their job much more effectively. There might not be enough public money—or, more to the point, public support—available for a replay!

During the boom period the last group, politicians, rode the crest of the popularity wave, and, when time was up, lived up to their age-old but unwritten motto, "our sole objective is to be reelected." So surely we are allowed to cry a little, particularly if now, in crystal-clear hindsight, we realize that perhaps we could have changed it all by our collective voting and consumer power. But we didn't change things, so things didn't change. We will pay for this collective oversight for quite some considerable time in increased taxes, higher banking fees, and rising interest rates.

WERE WE REALLY THAT GOOD? OR, KICK THE FAT CAT

One of the damaging side effects of the latest boom period, to my mind, has no doubt been the emergence of a class of senior managers, particularly in the financial services industry, who considered themselves exceptional. Therefore, they expected, demanded, and what's more, got outrageously large rewards. Ironically and almost perversely, if things didn't quite work out, these "unfortunates" still received remarkably generous termination payments. The major argument for this tsunami in reward schemes was that you couldn't hire outstanding people if you didn't match what others were prepared to pay. The argument changed from, "this person earns a lot because he is good" to "this person earns a lot so he must be good." This assertion was readily encouraged by a class of compensation consultants who got paid handsomely for this advice!

So the ridiculous situation developed that so-called superior talent got vast sums of money, regardless of their performance. Financial benefit was ensured no matter how dismal their decisions or poor the result of their actions were. But here's the paradox: If you take the personal risk out of management decision making, why would you worry at all whether your decisions were right or wrong? This suggests a true state of "tails you win, heads you don't lose." Unfortunately this state of affairs has consequences for the management population at large. If your boss appears to grab what he can, why shouldn't you? A whole culture of greed and "me first" has developed that has greatly increased the gap between the haves and the have-nots. The French revolution is an extreme historical example of what can happen as a consequence of such a culture. This grab-what-you-can management culture was supported, or perhaps even created, by our whole society's outlook on life, which has become focused in the extreme on materialism, pure greed, and the achievement of personal gain, whatever the cost.

Even BAD Practice Makes Perfect 1.1
Me First

A man and his girlfriend, in that order, are on a tandem bicycle enjoying a bicycle ride through the woods on what is obviously a fine summer evening. The tandem has a basket attached to the front handlebars, in which some snacks and drinks are carried. The man lifts out a wrapped bar, one of those that contains two pieces of candy, looks at the basket again, and realizes that this is the last bar. There's an overhanging tree branch on the path ahead. He turns his head and gives his girlfriend a wicked smile, then ducks. His girlfriend gets hit by the branch and falls off the bicycle. He carries on grinning triumphantly, while eating both pieces of candy.

One up for "me first"!

A young man and his girlfriend are seated in a movie theatre. It's a good movie, so their attention is wholly focused on the screen. Somewhat absentmindedly, he offers her a piece of candy from a packet. She accepts and mumbles thank you. Without letting his eyes wander from the screen, he reaches in the bag and discovers to his horror that he just offered her the last piece of candy. He looks at her sideways, notices her satisfied chewing motions, leans over, and kisses her full on the mouth. His kiss appears to increase in passion but in reality he forcefully sucks the piece of candy out of her mouth. He then returns his attention to the movie, chewing gratefully, while she is left looking bewildered with a puzzled and disgusted look.

Our "me first" hero wins again!

Both examples above were advertisements for very popular snack products screened extensively on European TV Networks.

So, at the lower end of the organizational spectrum, a situation has developed that is similar to that at the top. To further illustrate this argument, it is a well-known fact that about 80% of all of us think that we are well-above-average drivers. Also, and more to the point, each one of us is under the impression that he or she is much more productive than the average worker. And, on top of that, all of us are overconfident of winning in so-called winner-take-all scenarios.[9] The continuous emphasis that is being placed on individual behavior makes these misconceptions much more dangerous than they ever were before. The insistent requirement and need for technical skills and individual know-how at the expense of social skills reinforces the notion that we are special and therefore can aspire to star player status.

This manifestation is particularly evident in college and university graduates, if and when they enter the workplace for the first time. In Northern Europe, this highly educated generation, the age group from, say, 25 to 40, and thus the potential senior management group, is often referred to as the "holiday generation." They look for rewarding careers in respectable companies that provide short working hours with lots of time for hobbies and sports. They expect much and give relatively little. They tend to be individualistic, but they do not ask for help, and they do not give feedback. One of them, a very bright but cocky youngster with an MBA degree on which the ink had not yet dried, said to me a couple of years ago, "I'll give you what you want; just leave me to it!"

Some of them freely admit that their studies were concerned only with the transfer of knowledge, and that little or no time was spent on the acquisition of social skills. But if asked in job interviews, they all revert to standard answers such as hard worker, very sociable, get on well with people, like to be part of a team, and so forth. Large multinational companies have compensated for this lack of social skills by introducing lengthy internal training programs to teach the bright and beautiful how to work in teams and how to interact with clients. But the number of graduates who find places in large companies is relatively small, so most potential consultants and managers alike are not given the opportunity to acquire these skills early on in their career to the detriment of business in general and clients in particular.[10]

A GLUT OF CONSULTANTS

Easy pickings, often blatant management abdication, and perhaps some lack of internal skills have also led to an explosion of consultancy services. Particularly in large organizations and in government, the number of management consultants has skyrocketed. To put it bluntly, most people would get quite a shock to realize that a substantial amount of taxpayer money is spent on very well-paid consultants to let well-paid public servants off the hook. In large organizations, a similar picture emerges. Most large corporations are riddled with consultants who have infiltrated organizations at all levels. The hiring of consultants for a specific, well-defined task or project has become a thing of the past. Most consultants spend many years in large organizations on open-ended projects with continuously changing briefs. A business acquaintance of mine, an information business consultant, has spent the past ten years in a major European conglomerate on a number of interrelated projects that seem to be ongoing. The cost associated with these services is astronomical and almost belies the fact that the conglomerate in question has its own very large and well-staffed IT department! Unfortunately all these services make it too easy for managers to dodge their responsibilities and to hide behind expertise and opinions bought at a considerable price. The number of people who are telling management what it should be doing without taking responsibility and accountability for implementation and operation is becoming quite frightening. Not surprisingly, weak, or even worse lazy, management, if given half a chance, will hide behind this expertise, the more so if this advice is offered by the big names in the consultancy industries.

Individualism Reigns Supreme

Rewards in organizations have shifted more and more from the team and the financial period to the individual skill or even the individual deal. This focus on individualism has led to a short-term reward outlook that belies all the central management principles such as vision, corporate planning, and long-term survival. This approach does not even consider preparation for the ups and downs of business or building some reserves for a rainy day. The only common goal appeared to be that next month's or next quarter's results had to be even better than those of the previous month or quarter. Naturally, management was cheered on by this close-to-obsessive concentration on the short term by shareholders and their support troops, the ones who make a living from reporting what has happened, what is bound to happen, or what should happen—according to them anyway.

Who Takes Responsibility?

All the above developments led to a situation wherein managers did not feel responsible anymore for whatever they were supposed to be responsible for. So, although individual performance had to be rewarded lucratively, blame was shared among as many people as possible, preferably at as low a level as possible. The number of times in the past ten years that we saw high-powered CEOs and high-ranking government officials explaining publicly that they personally did not feel answerable for the latest mess up, but that they would do everything in their power to correct the situation, was quite disgusting, to me anyway.

So, to get back to the question, "Were we really that good?" my answer must be a resounding no. At best, most of us, managers I mean, were riding the crest of the wave created by the very system that has now (2009) collapsed spectacularly. It was easy access to cheap finance that indirectly, but also directly, generated a consumer spending boom second to none. Unfortunately, this boom was financed largely by debt, whole mountains of it, based on security that has since partly evaporated. Major adjustments will have to be faced, including perhaps a protracted period of declining demand and fierce competition. Therefore, an awful lot of current-day managers will have to come to grips with the uncomfortable fact that management in tough times is very different from that practiced in economic boom times. That's going to be some adjustment, believe you me!

SO LET'S TAKE STOCK AND GET ON WITH IT

At critical economic times, such as at the end of the latest boom period, it's always a good idea to pause, take stock, and evaluate our own current situation accurately. Perhaps three of the most obvious but often overlooked points that need to be touched on here before we move on are these:

1. Nobody knows what will happen next.
2. Historical parallels don't really work.
3. Paying attention to the stock market is not really helpful.

Fortunately we are not yet able to look into the future, although some experts or analysts will create the impression that they can. Listen politely, then get on with the day-to-day business. Unfortunately past trends no longer apply, and most companies will find themselves in uncharted waters. Forecasts, budgets, and predictions were all based on past trends and on a relatively stable and predictable environment, so forget them—they are no longer applicable—and concentrate primarily on the *now*. Also spend some time thinking and planning, if you can, on the longer term and its possible consequences for your products or services. During bust times, markets have a tendency to shake out truly mature products and favor untested but exciting totally new solutions. It's a time for renewal and for stimulating new opportunities!

The second item, to look for historical parallels and thus somehow find the answer to what is going to happen next, is a total waste of management time. The current bust cannot be compared with the 1929 crash, or with any other past downturn, for that matter. The current bust, and the next one, are the ones that present management, including you, will have to cope with; all previous crises are background noise, and they cannot possibly contribute to solving your problems now or to identifying future opportunities for your business.

The last item, the stock market, is difficult to ignore, but ignore it we must. The media are focused continually on the swings of the market. We are bombarded by authoritative and speculative opinions on a daily, sometimes hourly, basis as to why the market went up and why it crashed down again. Unfortunately the link between the real earnings of companies and share prices was severed long ago. If you want to bet on the mood swings of the market, go ahead, and be a trader. If you want to run a business, take no notice, and run a business!

Why Are *We* Still in Business?

With the above in mind, take a step back and evaluate your own current business situation as realistically and, most of all, as honestly as you can. What needs to be answered is the question, Why are we still in business? The premise is fairly straightforward as well; namely, as long as you exist as a business, you must be doing something right! If you know the answer to that question, so much the better.

If you don't, spend a bit of time evaluating your business with your senior management team. Look at sales and sales performance, customer complaints, competition, financial situation, cash flow, production, quality, logistics, after sales, service, and so forth. All the critical areas of your business need to be evaluated as to their current performance. If you want to use a rough rating system for evaluation purposes, just rate each parameter on a scale of one to four, with 1 representing *excellent,* 2 representing *good,* 3 representing *needs improvement,* and 4 representing *unacceptable.* Don't make it too complex, and try to use your existing reporting systems. After all, you should have some idea, for example, of the number of production rejects, delivery mess ups, the number of customer complaints, or other industry-significant parameters. Do all of this with the purpose of finding the answer to the question, Why are we still in business? If you know what you are doing really well, you can certainly make those things even better! It's the principle of building on your strengths. Normally to achieve that doesn't cost very much, and, it's almost guaranteed to be a lot cheaper than addressing the weak points of the organization. That can come later; after all, at the moment you are still on the field and in the game, whereas some competitors have already been forced to leave.

Focus

While this is going on, realize that you need to focus keenly on managing your own people and the business during a downturn. There is much to unlearn, relearn, and maybe just simply learn. If you as a manager accept that, you will actually enjoy the learning experience of a downturn, and you will be much the better manager for it! After all, boom times are relatively easy management-wise, but bust times are certainly going to separate the management competent from the management incompetent, or, if you like, the men from the boys, or the women from the girls. Individual performance must become a distant second to overall team performance because company survival has to take overall priority. The challenge is to achieve team status in as short a time span as possible. Downturns wait for no company, and it's easy to be left behind. So there is no time to lose!

Text Layout and the Ground Rules

This introduction will confidently shift the mind-set into ignoring general circumstances and firmly focus on ourselves as managers, and on our own environments. After all, most macroeconomic shifts are beyond our control, and they are sometimes beyond even central bank or government control. A macroeconomic correction is required, and it will occur!

In Chapter 2, we will look at a number of issues to help us get back to earth. These include attribution bias, self-styled knowledge work, the concept of service economies, worldwide competition, and management as a science or art. These issues are put in the context of a downturn and referred to as *reality checks*. Reality is often "put on hold" during a long boom period, but it will always get back at us when we least expect it.

Then the text moves on in Chapter 3 to relearning some basic and often forgotten skills. Particularly, the chapter propagates an emphasis shift of *me the brand* to *us the team*; modern *winner-take-all* scenarios are discussed, and cheap marketing tools are highlighted for customer retention and promoting *us the brand*. Don't forget, even small companies are a *brand* to their very own customers. Any brand, international, national, or local, is worth protecting and promoting. For the stakeholders, the stakes are the same even if the scale varies from thousands to trillions.

In Chapter 4 the emphasis is on what one can control during a serious downturn. Expert and other sideline advice, media focus, and expected trends need to be firmly relegated to the useful to know, but not directly usable category. Instead focus on customers, control of the real cash flow, the public profile, and staying the course are addressed in some detail.

Chapter 5 discusses both personal and business opportunities. There are plenty of opportunities: personal opportunities to strengthen or upgrade one's own management skills, and opportunities for the business in general. The latter are divided into internal opportunities, such as inverse marketing, differentiation, and innovation, and external ones, such as possible acquisitions and the consequences thereof.

The last chapter introduces the idea of *M-EBIT* as an easy aid to remind us of our overall responsibility as managers and general managers in particular. M-EBIT, as opposed to the financial concept of EBIT, stands for the Managerial EBIT, that is, Managing the Environment, one's Business, oneself (I), and the Team. All the challenges of the previous chapters are reiterated and summarized. After all, sound management must find a balance for paying attention to all the stakeholders of the business—maybe not in equal measures, but depending on the moment, each one of them must get attention so the business can survive and flourish.

To illustrate a particular point or to simply highlight a behavior, bad or good, the main text is interspersed with some stand-alone anecdotes, set as sidebars, and loosely referred to as *Practice Makes Perfect* or a similar expression. The earlier sidebar, numbered 1.1 and named, "Even BAD Practice Makes Perfect," is an example. Most of these are taken from my own encounters or experiences as a general manager who is mature enough, in an elderly sense, to have lived through a number of downturns on more than one continent. Maybe the downturns were not as severe as the present worldwide situation, but for the unfortunate participants and victims, any downturn is the worst ever until the next one appears to beat all previous ones. Nowadays, thanks to the media, we are always in the "world-beating record" mode, whether it is the weather, the stock market, the number of company failures, or the latest blockbuster movie.

At the end of each chapter, a point-by-point summary is given to drive home important concepts that were discussed in the text.

Even in difficult times it is important to see the lighter side of business. This is illustrated particularly in Appendix A. The story told there twists the well-known fairy tale of "Snow White and the Seven Dwarfs" into a modern-day version, namely, the ghastly consequences of so-called progress to an ultimate "services-only" society.

The Bottom Line

We spend the better part of our adult lives working in or at business, and we should never be overcome by negative downward emotional spirals. Indeed, I have always felt that even in tough times a smile or even a laugh goes much farther than another dour I-told-you-so treatise or statement. Also, there is a tendency in our society to obsessively strive for minimizing personal and business risk. As a result, certainly in difficult times, we look for someone or something to blame. After all, it should never have happened, and certainly it should never happen again. But risk is part of life and most definitely part of business life. Capitalism is not dead, it is just temporarily dazed and on hold. And let us not forget that without risk, people would lose the entrepreneurial spirit that has built many a company and, what is more, created and shaped great nations. Possibilities are unlikely to be generated by negative thoughts or by punishing the guilty—never mind how satisfying that might feel—so keep on looking for the positives and the possibilities in your own environment by using the general guidelines and hints given in this book. After all, how can you as a manager motivate and stimulate your team if you can't even motivate and stimulate yourself! So let's get on with it. Be resilient: first accept some home realities, and then get beyond them and start relearning some forgotten but essential management truths!

CHAPTER 2

A REALITY CHECK IS LONG OVERDUE

Reality is merely an illusion, albeit a very persistent one.
—*Albert Einstein (1879–1955)*

THE STREETS ARE NOT PAVED WITH GOLD

The first realization that needs to be hammered home is that many opportunities that presented themselves in boom times will dry up very quickly in times of economic crises. During the good times even the most common of business ventures, more-on-the-same-theme ventures, so to speak, appeared to blossom effortlessly. Demand was there, so more and more people started companies that were competing with existing ones and other start-ups with little or no differentiation in products or services offered. Particularly in industries with low entrance barriers, new ventures mushroomed.[1] But in boom times competition tends to deteriorate into what I would call pseudocompetition. Never mind how bad the service or even the product was; in the end there was always another customer. Stories of easy successes were on the front covers of local, national, and international newspapers and magazines. A lot of these laid-back start-ups will more than likely not survive the tough times because, even for the survivors, continuation will be a harsh struggle. Building and running a business can be a great deal of fun and extremely satisfying along the way, but it's never easy. Never has been, and never will be.

A Dearth of Customers

For companies that were well established before a boom started, to live through a serious downturn will be just as traumatic. Probably these companies would have experienced a relaxed time maintaining and even increasing profitability. Not much time had to be spent on retaining customers. In good times, a lot of products walk out of the door unaided, figuratively speaking.

Good times are not very conducive to preaching and practicing effective customer retention. After all, if it's far too easy to acquire customers, customer
retention is taken almost for granted. It's a sellers' market, with the buyers
falling over each other to get what they want at almost any cost, relatively
speaking. But when the tide has turned, the customer base shrinks, and
relentless price competition seems to be the order of the day, the concept of
retaining customers—never mind acquiring new ones—will really have to
be relearned. Companies and households alike have decided to stop playing
full-time for a while and take plenty of breaks; no one knows when full play
will be resumed and whether the order of play will be the same. Not many
companies have well-established, realistic plans for doomsday scenarios,
particularly after such a prolonged period of growth that we were fortunate
enough to experience from the mid-1980s well into 2008.[2]

Paradox of Thrift

A very powerful contradiction comes into play as well, namely, the
corporate version of the *paradox of thrift*.[3] It's best explained in this way:
Every company does what is prudent for itself but by, for example, reducing
its spending, it slows down the overall economy still further and thus harms
everyone, including ironically itself. Particularly the current crisis (2009),
frequently referred to as the "credit crunch," has illustrated this paradox
already for, in particular, the financial services, the transport, and the white
goods sectors. It might be ironic, but when demand starts slowing down, the
paradox is almost inevitable.

Safe Havens No More

In a serious downturn, a lot of safe havens are on hold too. Nothing
is safe anymore, not even your own dull and boring bank, let alone that
reliable large customer that always paid on time but has started dragging
its heels too. More and more customers will delay payments or even default
on them. Thus remind yourself of that often-forgotten truth—a sale is not
a sale until the cash is in your bank. Government contracts are perhaps an
exception to the above trend, but you might have to wait much longer for
payments due. Your bank probably won't want to finance those increased
working capital requirements either. It's not a good time to seek additional
finance for mundane things like day-to-day operating expenses. What's more,
additional capital requirements and funds for more exotic ventures will be
almost impossible to obtain, unless you can prove guaranteed returns and
adequate security.

JIT Is on Hold Too

The just-in-time, or, if you like, the ultra-lean supply chain is under severe strain as well. If your suppliers need to get paid immediately because they cannot get even the basic trade credit they were so used to, you have to put your own cash flow at risk in order to keep the inputs flowing that are a must-have for your own outputs. Particularly organizations with well-established but very complex supply links will find this a challenge and a half. Witness the car industry, where numerous small suppliers of minor but critical parts don't have the cushion to survive, hence jeopardizing the much larger client, the vehicle assembly plant.

All this then leads us to *Reality Check 1: the streets are no longer paved with gold. In actual fact, the open-for-business streets are full of potholes that have to be avoided in order to keep going at all. Even then it's going to be a bumpy ride!*

IN A MODERN KNOWLEDGE ECONOMY WE CAN EXIST BY PROVIDING SERVICES ONLY

A recession is a wonderful time to bring back reality to quite a number of predictions, theories, and even developments that started in boom times, but that have not as yet been tested as to their real validity. A major one that I find particularly intriguing is the linked notion of a services economy based on information of latter-day knowledge, combined with the notion of the *knowledge worker.*

An Economy Based on Services Only?

For those of us who have been around for a while, it's all rather confusing. We were just getting used to the real benefits of the industrial era when the next major development phase began rapidly engulfing our familiar environment. Skeptically inclined readers can be forgiven also. After all, "the new economy" in the mid-1990s that was forever going to change our perception of the words *profit* and *shareholder value* proved to be nothing more than a latter-day version of *tulip mania.*[4] Investment *burn rate* became a fashionable concept and, for a short time anyway, indicative of success. Logically, and not in hindsight this time, profit survived as a business concept, and predictably a lot of small-time investors were brought back to earth with the proverbial thud. Similarly an expression such as *postcapitalist society* can only bring a wry smile to all faces that have seen an increase in income disparity to dizzy, beyond vulgar levels, particularly in the last ten years or so, between top management and the remainder of the troops in a lot of industries. The expression "grab-what-you-can society" would not sound as grand, but it would certainly be more descriptive of recent trends in what appears to be acceptable, to be aspired to, and even to-be-admired human behavior. So are we in for another craze invented by academia, consultants, and human oracles and fuelled by the popular press, like so many others? Or can we really talk about a major shift in the basics underlying our modern-day (2009) Western economies? And is it really possible to have a society or country where everyone is associated with services only, from cleaning offices to expensive advisory services and software development? Let us examine this notion in a bit more detail, starting with the managerial know-how associated with modern-day manufacturing.

Hard-Earned Managerial Know-How

If we believe the explosion of academic and popular articles in the 1980s, 1990s, and even more recently, we find ourselves on the verge of a brand-new era. From industrialism to postindustrialism to "new economy" to knowledge or information economy, all in a matter of a decennium or two is no mean feat for humankind, particularly if seen in the context of our known historical advances. Are we really experiencing an ever-accelerating development phase in which science and technology are progressing beyond industrialism, that is, manufacturing, to a new Promised Land of generating useful output via knowledge and services only? Particularly in the Western world, the number of people employed in industry has steadily declined over the past forty years, whereas the number of people employed in services has increased dramatically.[5]

There are plenty of renowned economists and management gurus who, on the basis of these facts, have made cases for the evolving importance of so-called knowledge work, almost exclusively associated with business services only, and the emerging knowledge or information society. Fortunately there have also been a few dissenting voices. They have seriously questioned our almost "good riddance, let's be done with it" attitude to the accelerating swap of an advanced manufacturing environment to the "Promised Land of information services," devoid of grubby tasks such as manufacturing and distribution. But, is it really that clever to exchange real technological know-how, acquired over many generations in industries with very, *very* high entrance barriers to services or software industries whose entrance barriers are generally speaking pretty minimal? And what about the consequences for management practices? Eamon Fingleton wrote,

> A key point here is that the managerial challenge of running a software company is not nearly as daunting as is generally imagined, and it is certainly modest compared to running an efficient manufacturing

business. Whereas the production flow in a modern First World factory may have to be coordinated on a split-second basis (think of the just-in-time inventory control system in the automobile industry), software work generally involves few truly critical deadlines; typically there is just one, the deadline by which the entire program must be finished. Thus, although the success of top manufacturing companies like Toyota and Daimler-Benz stems in large measure from a sophisticated management culture that has taken several decades to hone, software firms need no similarly deep management tradition to succeed.

In short, as the Silicon Valley venture capitalist Donald Valentine has pointed out, software is "a simple business." Given that Valentine helped create such phenomenally successful ventures as Cisco Systems, Oracle, and 3-Com, he should know. Speaking of his habit of investing large amounts of money in software start-ups run by untried young entrepreneurs, Valentine says of the software industry: "Twenty-three-year-olds can figure it out. If it were a complicated business like a steel mill, with unions and all this material coming all the time and two shifts, I might want older people with experience."[6]

Hard-hitting words written by what appears to be a "voice in the wilderness" in defense of hard industries and management skills developed over many years of incremental technical know-how and managerial maturing.

Postindustrialists tend to define manufacturing as a labor-intensive and unsophisticated activity of the assembly type. What they appear to overlook is that assembly is the last and often the least-complicated step in the making of a modern consumer good. Earlier steps, such as the manufacture of components and materials, are more than often highly sophisticated, not to forget the manufacture of production machines, those that actually make these components and materials. Modern manufacturing industries require large amounts of capital and proprietary production knowledge that are not so easy to acquire and that are even more difficult to copy. In contrast, postindustrial or knowledge services do not require large amounts of capital nor much proprietary know-how. In fact, most of the necessary know-how can be acquired from public or semipublic sources, thanks to the principle of knowledge intensity.[7] Significant shifts in employment from manufacturing to services do have as a consequence the subsequent loss of technological and managerial know-how that were the root of our modern-day management culture. Also, as there appeared to be little future in manufacturing, the bold and the bright opted for careers in service or, if you like, knowledge industries. Between 35 and 45% of all business school graduates alone were absorbed by the financial services industry in 2008.[8]

Services and Knowledge Organizations

There is no doubt that increases in commerce and trade have required the financial services sector to expand. But it is also true that the increase in useful services has been well overtaken by the "invention" of very lucrative activities that benefited this sector only. The financial services sector ranked second only to the computer software industry in the praise showered upon it by the proponents of the knowledge economy. Unfortunately, as we now (2009) know, many of the financial sector's fastest-growing activities turned out to be utterly unproductive and even positively destructive from the point of view of the economy.

Another derivative of the almost frenzied buildup created around knowledge as one of the main drivers of the economy is the term *knowledge organization*, or *knowledge-based businesses*.[9] It is not quite clear, to me anyway, what actually sets these types of businesses apart from, presumably, nonknowledge organizations or nonknowledge-based businesses. Again, the argument that knowledge is but one of the parameters important in a knowledge-based economy, coupled to the fact that knowledge is a continuum in the development of our economy, makes these terms somewhat pretentious. To my way of thinking, all businesses are knowledge based, and all progress, in most if not all industries, has relied heavily on the development of technology. Naturally some businesses will depend more on technology than others, but where the boundary lies between knowledge and other organizations must be, to say the least, difficult to determine, and what's more to the point, most probably of little use. Just because some companies employ rooms full of people sitting behind computers, either inputting or manipulating information, does not necessarily rank them as a knowledge organization. Again the danger is that a modern car-manufacturing plant is classed as *industrial* and an applied software-development company as *knowledge*. Which one of the two organizations is better for the overall economy, taking into consideration supplier industries, number of employees, and service opportunities? On top of that we should ask ourselves, in which one of these organizations is more valuable, difficult to acquire, or technically sophisticated knowledge locked in?

Is Knowledge Related to Services Only?

The sometimes proposed conclusion that a knowledge economy is in essence a services economy is particularly dangerous. In *A Primer on the Knowledge Economy*, by Houghton and Sheehan, the authors write,

At the core of the economy are goods producing industries, linked into value chains which see inputs coming from knowledge-based

business services and goods related construction and energy industries, and outputs going to goods related distribution service
industries.[10]

Industries concerned with the creation, production, and distribution of
goods (including manufacturing) remain at the heart of the economy.

Thus, a simplistic interpretation of a structural economic shift from
manufacturing to services, that is, from industrial era to knowledge economy,
does not really do justice or reflect the increasingly complex chain from raw
materials via production and distribution to global consumer. It is as well to
remember that! After all, in the end it is the consumption of physical products that really drives the world economy.

Negroponte, on a similar topic of finding the rightful place of information
in today's world, writes in an essay entitled "Bits and Atoms,"

> The information superhighway is about the global movement of
> weightless bits at the speed of light. As one industry after another
> looks at itself in the mirror and asks about its future in a digital
> world, that future is driven almost 100 percent by the ability of
> that company's product or services to be rendered in digital form.
> If you make cashmere sweaters or Chinese food, it will be a long
> time before we can convert them to bits. "Beam me up, Scotty" is a
> wonderful dream, but not likely to come true for several centuries.
> Until then you will have to rely on FedEx, bicycles, and sneakers to
> get your atoms from one place to another. This is not to say that
> digital technologies will be of no help in design, manufacturing, and
> management of atom-based businesses. I am only saying that the core
> business won't change and your product won't have bits standing in
> for atoms.[11]

Fingleton puts it even more strongly in his premise that our Western love
affair with service industries will put us in danger of "losing not only our
shirts but our pants as well." He refers to the new wave of knowledge and
services as postindustrialism and writes,

> Not only do those who advocate postindustrialism overestimate the
> prospects for postindustrial services, but they greatly underestimate
> the prospects for manufacturing. A major problem with the argument
> of postindustrialists is that they do not understand how sophisticated
> modern manufacturing truly is.[12]

Can Services Survive on Their Own?

What must remain is the notion that modern manufacturing businesses were and still are based on very complex and diverse sets of knowledge. This type of deep-rooted and often painfully acquired knowledge is not so easily transmitted as some types of modern-day services knowledge. It is difficult to envisage an economy totally geared to so-called high-level services.[13] It is difficult particularly because it is exactly those services that travel well and that are easily duplicated in other locations without large investments in capital, unlike their manufacturing counterparts. It's not unlike the employee-versus-consumer controversy of the late fifties. As an employee, a Western industrial worker demanded all the benefits and security that an organization and society could provide, but as a consumer he wanted keenly priced consumer goods. So he worked for Phillips during the day and watched his Sony TV at night or worked for General Motors and drove a Honda. What is stopping the nations that still possess real manufacturing capabilities from closing down the services in the Western world and doing it themselves for half the price? While they acquire and absorb the difficult process of manufacturing management know-how, we are willing to trade it for the much simpler skills of services management.

A fairy-tale look at what could happen if the balance between value adding and service industries shifts relentlessly to the latter is illustrated in Appendix A, "Snow White and The Seven Dwarfs, or the Result of an Ultimate Service Economy." Could this be our destiny too? In Appendix B, some further thoughts are given to this intriguing concept of knowledge economy and knowledge workers and the possible consequences of too much emphasis on services, not on real added-value industries.

Reality Check 2: After the spectacular implosion of the financial services sector, let's not bet all our hard-earned knowledge on a service economy only.

What Then Comes after Service Industries?

The large social problem of considering what will happen to all the people who cannot lay claim to, or who are unsuited to, so-called knowledge work is often ignored by the proponents of a purely services or knowledge economy. And what comes after services? In an article entitled, "White Collars Turn Blue," Krugman paints a gloomy picture:

Most important of all, the prophets of an information economy seem to have forgotten basic economics. When something becomes abundant, it also becomes cheap. A world awash in information will be a world in which information per se has very little market value. And in general, when the economy becomes extremely good at doing something, that activity becomes less rather than more important. Late 20th-century America was supremely efficient at growing food. That was why it had hardly any farmers. Late 21st-century America is supremely efficient at processing routine information; that is why the traditional white-collar worker has virtually disappeared from the scene.[14]

What is a knowledge worker anyway—a modern-day computer operator, a business or financial analyst, or just a postindustrial employee suffering from title delusion?

KNOWLEDGE WORKERS ARE A UNIQUE BAND OF BROTHERS

If you firmly believe that we have arrived in a distinct knowledge era, then naturally you need to stock it with knowledge workers![15] After all, what's knowledge if there are no workers to cultivate, promote, and practice it? The magic question that literally begs for an answer is of course, what exactly is a knowledge worker? Is it a generic term that covers all types of work, or has the term been hijacked by the information and communication technology (ICT) industry to "rename their workers" in order to give them that extra cachet that falls squarely in the category of title inflation or attention grabbing?[16] Certainly, the majority of publications and Web sites relating to the subject imply that knowledge workers are exclusive to the information processing industry. One can almost sense the satisfaction between the lines that "their industry" [ICT] has come of age and is now at the forefront of our economic development, ignoring the blip caused by the financial-services sector of course. So a knowledge worker is purported to be a latter-day back-room nerd, but with a more socially acceptable and certainly more exciting sounding label. Is this a true reflection of what a knowledge worker should or shouldn't be? And more to the point, what exactly is knowledge work?

What Is Knowledge Work?

Kit Sims Taylor recognized six more or less distinct types of knowledge work, namely,

1. Routine work that would be hard to separate from knowledge work. For example, formatting and beautifying text is done by most knowledge workers, as typists and secretaries are a dying breed.

2. Networking, promoting, and socializing. This falls squarely in the category of vague but sometimes useful activities.
3. Finding the data or information needed to produce the knowledge. Some skill required to use search engines effectively.
4. Creating what others, quite frequently, have created already because producing it would take less time than searching for it.
5. Creating what has not been created before. Real original knowledge work.
6. Communicating what has been learned or produced.[17]

The distinction between items 4 and 5 is of critical importance. Most so-called creative work is reinventing the wheel, and *re-creation* would be a better description of most knowledge activities. Taylor expounded on this some more as follows,

> The fate of most knowledge workers is a work life in which we are constantly reinventing the exam question, the flood insurance clause, the advertising copy for a sweater ad—producing goods and services that are new to us but not new to the greater society. Such work may well be pleasant and fulfilling. The knowledge worker is indeed engaged in the creation of knowledge. But the knowledge worker is being paid for it only because creating knowledge that exists elsewhere is presently cheaper than finding it.[18]

The obvious danger to a knowledge economy is that the more accessible knowledge developed by a knowledge worker becomes, the less need there is for the re-creation of the same knowledge by other knowledge workers.

A second item that is often overlooked by most of the enthusiastic supporters of a services economy consisting of large numbers of knowledge workers is what Taylor calls the "analog backlog." A lot of business data and data in general was and still is in analog form. Thus large staffs of analog-to-digital translators, or what could be called lower-level knowledge workers, are needed to get this information into digital form. This group of knowledge workers, the modern-day version of the assembly line worker, or "keyboard slaves" is probably better educated than his industrial counterpart but still trapped in the monotony of mostly repetitive work. Naturally there are new industries, such as the Web-hosting outfits that were not even dreamed of 20 years ago. But make no mistake about it—most of these are fast becoming basic services industries not unlike the energy giants that fuelled the industrial revolution.

Can Knowledge Workers Be Uniquely Identified?

On one Web site, knowledge workers were divided into "core" and "everyone else."[19] Examples of core knowledge workers were given as chief information or knowledge officers, knowledge managers, librarians, content managers, information officers, knowledge analysts, and so forth. The rest of the staff of this organization, the National Health Service in the United Kingdom, the people who actually do the work, I might add, like doctors, nurses, technicians, and so forth, were naturally classed as "everyone else." So the "guardians" of common, as opposed to individual, knowledge are core to knowledge workers, whereas the "generators and users" are everyone else? A peculiar way of looking at knowledge to my mind! We used to call it filing and document control! However, that is not the only Web site that "segments" knowledge workers. Categories such as functionalists, cube captains, nomads, global collaborators, and so forth, are really getting down to it. Yes sir, it's a whole new ball game out there, and all the positions and the labels are up for grabs!

If you take the time to search the Web for definitions of knowledge worker, you will come across the most wide-ranging, sometimes intriguing, and often bizarre definitions that bring you no farther along in your quest for what it is these "elusive" workers actually do. My all-time favorite appeared as a remark on a Web site called knowledgeboard.com, posted by an unknown correspondent. It reads as follows: "I suspect that the lack of focus on the

---

Practice Makes Perfect 2.1
The Knowledge

Long before the debate about knowledge work and knowledge workers even erupted, there was knowledge that was referred to as "The Knowledge" by the system that required candidates to acquire it.

If one wanted a license as a London cabbie in England, one had to pass a very elaborate and comprehensive test on getting around and knowing the streets of London like the back of one's hand. An aspiring cab driver would practice for this ultimate street knowledge test by crisscrossing the streets of London on a bicycle with a map on a clipboard attached to the handle bars. Needless to say, by the time he passed the test (often several attempts were required) a "graduate" London Cab driver really knew his City. London Cabbies were justifiably proud of this, "The Knowledge." Many a visitor in the 1970s and 1980s can attest to that! Ah, those good old days before the GPS made it possible for all of us to find our way around and still get lost!

---

issue of 'the individual knowledge worker' comes as a result of the specific characteristics of the work they do. Knowledge work is discretionary and invisible, thus difficult to identify and difficult to control."[20]

In its usual efficient bureaucratic manner, the United States Army produced a report entitled, "Evaluating Knowledge Worker Productivity: Literature Review," in 1994.[21] Its main conclusions were that measurement techniques must be tailored to fit the organization, and that the work to be analyzed should be classified by its components so the measurement technique's applicability can be evaluated. As was to be expected, "knowledge worker" performance is far too generic a term to be of any use whatsoever.

Sometimes the term knowledge worker is explained in such general terms that everyone bar the village idiot qualifies as a knowledge worker.[22] For example this one was found on a Web site that shall remain anonymous: "a worker who adds value by processing existing information to create new information which could be used to define and solve problems." Or this description: "someone whose knowledge and ability to learn is critical to what they do, even if they do it with their hands."[23] Are we getting any closer in deciding who is or who isn't a knowledge worker?

There is no doubt in my mind that the vast majority of what really should be considered part of the knowledge workers group was pretty well using knowledge as the basis of their daily work anyway. Perhaps the reason why the discussion of who is and who isn't a knowledge worker has remained with academia and with the ICT industry is that engineers have no real desire to be reclassified as knowledge workers, nor have nurses, doctors, lawyers, accountants, editors, economists, service technicians, and so forth. After all, it adds nothing to their status or recognition, and it reduces pretty specific disciplines into a broad category that serves no purpose whatsoever.

Postknowledge Debate

Much more pertinent than debating the merits of classifying employees into knowledge and presumably nonknowledge categories are the youngest members of the workforce born in the 1980s and 1990s. This generation has been called by social researchers "the Millennials," "Generation Y," or "the Net Geners," short for Net Generation, for obvious reasons.[24] The global downturn must have been a rude awakening for this generation. Born in an age of plenty, with jobs easy to get and job hopping even easier, a lot of them are now (2009) experiencing a brutal awakening with their jobs actually disappearing; historically, in a downturn the youngest part of the work force always suffers the most. For the ones who remain in jobs, dramatic changes will take place as well. Among themselves they talk about "pressure cookers," "boiler rooms," and "slave labor" in describing their changed working environments. The free, open, and collaborative style that they enjoyed so much is rapidly being replaced by a command-and-control approach, particularly in firms struggling to survive. Fortunately they are also the most adaptive part of the population, and they will probably adjust pretty quickly to more Spartan living conditions and a harsher business environment.

In conclusion, knowledge economy and knowledge workers are concepts that are inclined to endanger our perception of what really adds value in an economy. *Therefore, Reality Check 3 must be the realization that no one in a business team is above tangible contribution to output. Let's bid farewell to the vague concept of knowledge workers and extend a warm welcome to Net Geners!*

ATTRIBUTION BIAS AND STAR INDULGENCE ARE WIDESPREAD

Particularly during boom times the phenomenon referred to as "attribution bias" surfaces big-time. Attribution bias is defined as the tendency of people to credit themselves unduly with successes that are heavily influenced by external factors, such as a boom market or a technology revolution, while disproportionately blaming their failures on external factors.[25]

Thus a prolonged period of unprecedented growth will have inflated quite a few management egos, sometimes to the point of overinflation and destruction! When boom turns to bust, the same egos refuse to admit that failure was also part of their very own "skill" set. Unfortunately, we all suffer from attribution bias to a greater or lesser extent. Hence there must be a lot of managers around who think that their alleged superior management skills or expertise during the boom period was what created success in the first place. Sadly, attribution bias is most definitely not congenial to humility or to sound management practices. On the contrary, to manage effectively during hard times is the real test for anyone's management skills. It's like life itself: it's the tough times that really develop resilience and shape character. Naturally no one, including the writer, wishes hard times on societies in general and on managers in particular, but a better awareness of attribution bias might help to put easy boom-time achievements into perspective.

Star Players?

Closely associated with attribution bias is the *star player* syndrome that has really come into its own devastating effect. Like attribution bias, the very concept of the modern star player is based on the individual, without considering the environment or, dare we say it, the team in which the star player operates. All is concentrated on the notion of oneself and the terrific achievements that can be or are attributed to individuals without due consideration of support, backup, or even teamwork.

In every organization there are employees who do a better job than their peers. One of management's tasks has always been to recognize superior ability and, if possible, nurture and develop it to facilitate succession and provide for the next generation of senior management. Often these employees were referred to as high flyers or high potentials.[26] They were given every opportunity to broaden their skills in the various aspects of the business over a number of years. The desire of every ambitious young executive was to climb that corporate ladder. After all, the traditional job evaluation schemes were geared toward more pay for more responsibility in terms of people, assets, or both. Specialists, the essential backroom men and women, the research scientists, engineers, cost accountants, highly skilled technicians, and so on and so forth, were often ignored in this race to the top and left somewhere in the middle ranks to sit out their tenure. Now it was also true that most real specialists, the ones I have come across, anyway, really enjoyed their work, thrived on mental challenges and had no desire to climb the corporate management ladder and waste their time on political intrigue and power play, although they would have enjoyed a bit more money and recognition, no doubt. They get their own recognition and power from their association with professional bodies and their counterparts working for other, sometimes even competing, organizations.

Loyalty No More

Both categories of employees, the high flyers and the specialists, were often extremely loyal to their organization, and in return the organization gave them security of tenure. This traditional band was broken some time ago when commercial pressures kept on increasing relentlessly, and shareholders, driven on by the market, expected ever-improving company results. Enter the era of reengineering, downsizing, outsourcing, and so forth; a much more unstable environment to cultivate and nurture long-term employee relations.

In return, employees became more mercenary, and if they did not get what they wanted in the short term, they were quite prepared to seek their fortunes somewhere else. While more and more mission statements and corporate visions started sprouting the slogans, "our people are our best resource," and more and more money was spent on all the human resource techniques, such as succession planning, training, improving working conditions, you name it, more and more employees voted with their feet for a few dollars more. Equally, only lip service was paid to these noble-sounding statements preached by senior management. It was almost as if the more you spoke and wrote about it, the less you had to practice it. Long-term considerations were not appreciated by the market in the guise of analysts, brokers, investment bankers, and other financial wizards who were involved in an almost minute-by-minute monitoring of company stock fortunes. Private companies were dragged along as well. After all, laggards were losers.

Loyalty went out the door, and selfishness and greed became very acceptable traits on the part of employer and employee alike. This trend was obviously more evident as practiced from the, top but it was just as pronounced lower down, recognizable by subtle, or sometimes not-so-subtle, means, such as "sick" days, frequent and widespread Web surfing, game playing on company time, extended smoke breaks, lengthy private telephone calls and endless private e-mail correspondence.

To put not too fine a point to it, our Western society had become one in which selfishness and greed were practiced, nurtured, admired, and aspired to by quite a few of us. It's not surprising that initial calls by government and organizations alike to beat this (2009) pretty serious downturn with slogans, such as "we are all in this together," "we need to pull together," or "we are all on the same team," do not have the instant and urgently desired effect. After years of grazing in the green pastures of ever-increasing profits, salaries, and, in the case of governments, tax receipts, a major adjustment is required. Bloated government and staff departments need to be trimmed. But in particular, public and private management needs to abandon self-centeredness and star-seeking behavior and rediscover its main (or maybe even its supreme and only) task—surprisingly enough, management! We really have to rediscover the art of managing people in teams, developing team spirit, giving credit to the team, and rediscovering the phrase, "If it wasn't for my team, we would have never achieved what we did achieve."

Reality Check 4 is that you can't change from blatant individualism to team play and social awareness in one slick, easy move.

THE SCIENCE OF MANAGEMENT?

The emphasis on individuals and individual performance has had its effects on management practices as well. Ever since Taylor started his *time and motion* studies at the Midvale steelworks in Philadelphia, the argument of whether management is an art or a science has swung like a pendulum between the two.[27] The science part is obviously much more structured than the art part, and the former can be taught pretty effectively and, what is more to the point, practiced almost immediately. Therefore, it's not surprising that in an age of sophisticated business systems, intra- and extranets, chat and blog sites, and so forth, management training has tended toward the science part at the expense of the art or soft side. Couple to this the industries that absorbed most business graduates, namely, management consultancies and the financial services industry, and you must concentrate training on analytical skills at the expense of people-management skills. After all, business schools adjust their offerings to their key clients, too. The theory of social and people-management skills, the arty part, was introduced all right, but it can be developed only by on-the-job training and real-life experiences. Naturally, but of critical importance, the right setting is required as well. The aforementioned service industries are hardly a multidimensional training environment for all-around management skills. Only after quite some time in actual relevant practice is the correct balance found between hard and soft skills.

Mentoring and Social Skills

In the armed forces, the inexperience in soft skills of junior officers has always been compensated in what one could call "the overlap principal." Although a recently graduated Army lieutenant is the de facto leader of a platoon, a unit of about 20 persons, later on in life most Army officers will admit that it was the platoon sergeant who really ran the unit. And many a colonel wouldn't know what to do without his regimental sergeant major! Indeed, there are few generals who did not start their careers in the forces as humble lieutenants who had to go through the mill to achieve their current status—truly a career and learning curve spread out over a life time. As not-for-profit organizations, the armed forces can afford to practice this extremely valuable and well-established on-the-job education program. Former middle and senior armed forces officers fit easily into industry management ranks.

Most commercial organizations have gone through an opposite development pattern. Relentless commercial pressure has had the exact contrary effect and removed layer upon layer of middle management in order for the company to remain competitive. Short of allocating a suitable mentor to a promising young manager or sending him on a basic course to practice interaction with his peers—who more than likely suffer from the same disability—little is actually done to alleviate the lack of down-to-earth skills so necessary in the practice of day-to-day management. One of my favorite notions that "the more we talk about critical issues, the less we actually do about them" holds true for the practice of interaction or social skills as well.[28] This lack of social skills is further magnified by the increasing sophistication of computer systems in transferring and dissecting information and generating reports. If you can get the information via "the system" at your very own desk in the safety of your very own office, what's the point of actually interacting with subordinates? Far too complicated!

In my own experiences in the past 10 years or so, I've come across a production manager who spent five and a half days out of six behind his computer and half a day with his five supervisors in his own office. He was

---

Practice Makes Perfect 2.2
A Targeted Learning Experience

In the early 1980s in a large retail chain, I had the privilege as part of my duties to run what was called the *retail development program*, or RDP for short. This program was run once a year in eight arduous weeks for 20 promising employees of this particular company. The RDP itself was run in the evening hours and on weekends. The preparation and execution of this program took well over a day a week for six months. It started with a preselection process by line and personnel managers to shortlist 100 potential candidates; total organizational strength at the time was in the region of 15,000. All of this took place in the strictest confidence.

Then, over a period of three months, the list was culled down to 30 employees by a committee consisting of the divisional directors and me. These 30 employees were informed of their selection, interviewed at length, and then asked to decide whether they wanted to take part in the program. The offer was put in writing, and candidates had to respond formally within three days. Of the 30 candidates interviewed, up to five tended to withdraw for whatever reasons. One thing was certain: during eight grueling weeks, there was not much time for fun, family life, or other leisure pursuits. Then a final selection was made to arrive at the magic number of 20. Four groups of five candidates each were formed. The ones who were interviewed but not selected, and who had not withdrawn, were almost guaranteed a second chance the following year, all things, in particular personal performance, being equal. Then four mentors, one for each group, were selected from the senior management ranks. Mentors were also interviewed and had to commit to be available after working hours and weekends for the eight-week period. It was considered quite an honor to be selected as a mentor. The main task of mentors was to challenge the group in its discussions and deliberations, but not to take part directly.

On a general note, all senior managers were encouraged to write up specific, practical cases at all times. This meant that there was always a good supply of these cases available. They were converted to case studies by one of the training managers on a regular basis. Every year, eight case studies covering the main areas of the company were selected for that particular RDP. The four groups were assigned a case each week on Monday. The suggestions for the case were to be presented on Saturday afternoon. Each group got one hour to present its analysis and recommendations. Marks were awarded after all groups were heard by a panel of judges who consisted of the managing director, two of the divisional directors, and me. After completing all eight cases, candidates were awarded their RDP diplomas; failure was not an option. The actual cost of this program was absolutely minimal. Only one full-time admin assistant was employed. Commitment and time spent by management was considered part of managers' duties. The program certainly helped to shape much better all-around managers, esprit de corps—particularly among the graduates—and a greater awareness of the total business, instead of blindered departmental thinking.

---

a virtual stranger on the factory floor, and the workers just about stared him out of the place when he did make a quick trip to the floor!

Or, in a different setting a sales manager who was convinced that he could manage the overall sales from his office via his 10 area representatives, their daily e-mail reports, and his own generated weekly statistics, supplemented by industry figures obtained from the World Wide Web. After observing this for a short time and meeting with each representative in the field, it became clear to me that he was actually afraid to face his own subordinates. He was afraid to interact, respond to, and, perish the thought, perhaps even be criticized by them. Much safer to deal with the reports, e-mails, and phone calls screened by his secretary in the relative safety of his own office and behind his own screen. The added value of this type of management to an organization is nil, zilch, nothing—or perhaps even negative.

All this emphasis on modern scientific management and the lack of on-the-job training for interactive skills has not prepared the present-day manager for vague but critical issues such as setting realistic objectives, motivating the team in hard times, knowing what each member of the team is capable of, who can stay and who will be laid off in a downturn, how to get employees to take on more work at the same pay, how to correct disruptive behavior, how to correct bad work practices in a positive manner, and so forth.

*Reality Check 5 is to identify the practical shortcomings in current manage-
ment and to come to the realization that the business's only chance of survival is
to really start managing "the team."*

Reality Checks Summarized

1. The streets are no longer paved with gold. The remaining streets are
   full of potholes that have to be avoided in order to keep going at all.
   Bumpy ride ahead!
2. Let's not bet all our hard-earned knowledge on a service economy
   only.
3. Never mind worker labels; no one on a team is above tangible work
   output.
4. You can't change from blatant individualism to team play and social
   awareness in one slick, easy move.
5. Identify your practical shortcomings and start managing the team.

CHAPTER 3

WHAT HAS TO
BE RELEARNED

I am always ready to learn, although I do not like being taught.
—Winston Churchill (1874–1965)

WINNER-TAKE-ALL: A CONSEQUENCE OF GLOBALIZATION

Surviving a recession revolves around customers, your own staff, your environment, and some basic management principles. But let's start first of all by stating that for each individual company there is no such thing as *The Economy*. Particularly during a recession, one is bombarded by news about the economy this and the economy that, the currency something else, and the other thing on top of all that. Get used to putting all that information into an offline file marked "useful background" and start concentrating on "Your Economy," meaning your market and your customers. That is difficult enough in a modern global or near-global marketplace, where competition can come from far and wide, and winner-take-all is more often than not the only game in town.

The concept of winner-take-all and winner-take-all economies has been around for some time mainly thanks to—or no thanks to, depending on your point of view—the World Wide Web and advances in global communication and distribution.[1] Whether these possibilities provide us with more choice or with ultimate confusion still remains to be seen, but the concept of winner-take-all is of great interest, because it will affect your company's chances in the marketplace. The most characteristic feature of winner-take-all is that it translates small differences in performance into large differences in economic rewards. In adverse conditions such as the current (2009) worldwide financial crisis, this could very well spell disaster for quite a few companies that were doing quite okay in a mature, oversupplied market, due to pretty easy boom conditions. So the concept was probably parked during the boom times, but it will resurface quite strongly in a downturn. A winner-take-all scenario will most probably divide the world market into real global players, niche players for global markets, and regional players for regional markets. Strictly local players, such as the corner drugstore, the local garage, the single repairman, and so forth, fulfill a strictly local need, but they could be under threat when a chain business that provides the same service or products opens up in the neighborhood. However, local businesses tend to have a very faithful clientele that will keep on coming back because of their unique social neighborhood function and often supreme personalized service. Often, these businesses cease to exist when the owner decides to stop trading.

Regional players are of interest to global players because of their noticeable market share. Any attempt by regional players to become global players will be punished or rewarded, depending on whether an existing global player will viciously attack and destroy, or take over and absorb the regional player, respectively. The first alternative is bad for all participants in the unfortunate target company, whereas the latter tends to be good news for owners, but bad news for management and sometimes staff.

Consequences of Globalization

Globalization and winner-take-all are pretty well linked and cognizance has to be taken of the consequences of globalization, such as the following ones:

- Competition, even for niche products, takes place in the world market.
- Capital resources are moved across borders and at will.
- Production is rationalized on a global scale.
- Protecting domestic markets is increasingly difficult and often futile.
- Increased specialization resulting in an ever-greater complexity of production and distribution coordination sets the entrance barriers higher and higher.
- Time is becoming really important for competitiveness. In other words, windows of opportunity might be opened only very briefly before they are shut firmly.[2]

Against this background, it is quite instructive, but also crucial, to evaluate your own company and place it in the *global, niche global, regional,* or *strictly local* spectrum. Your company's position in the spectrum could very well determine its chances of survival. Regional companies are very much at risk during a downturn because they tend not to have the sales muscle, financial staying power, or access to government support to survive difficult times. If a multinational produces a product that achieves the same benefit for the customer as its regional counterpart, a price war is the best you can hope for! Global companies will look for an increase in market share during tough times in order to get those economies of scale really working for them. That's winner-take-all in practice. The only chance for regional companies lies in product differentiation and product innovation. As a matter of course, these should be the lifeblood of all small-to-medium regional companies anyway. Don't forget, product differentiation also means the simple marketing techniques introduced in the following section. There are plenty of examples of relatively small retailers that have piggybacked successfully on the anchor tenant(s) of large shopping malls. But you have got to be price competitive or truly unique or, alternatively, offer superior service or other real or perceived benefits.

Niche Global

Niche global companies should have a tremendous advantage in a downturn. Times will get tough or even tougher, but your products, know-how, and so forth, should stay distinctive and in demand, albeit at a reduced level for a while. For global niche players, the main emphasis should be on seeking cost reductions in their worldwide manufacturing and distribution costs. That is no mean feat against a background of tighter credit, strained cash flows, and decreases in demand. As a matter of course, innovation and differentiation must continue as even exclusive know-how will spread like wildfire. Remember the unique characteristics of *knowledge distribution* discussed previously.[3] These should include continuous innovation, exceptional quality, and a near-perfect Web site that is easy to find for the Web searcher in as many languages as practicable. This means a Web site that is easy and clear to navigate and that offers various ways to proceed with contact, such as e-mail, phone-back reminders, and brochure downloads. Prompt response to queries and a well-developed distribution network are a must as well.

Particularly niche global companies must be on the constant lookout for competitors starting up in faraway places. A continuous Web watch is a must to be aware of potential competitors and market developments.

Large Global

Large global companies in trouble attract government attention and frequently get support. Whether this is right or wrong is a moot point, but not altogether immaterial. After all, propping up a failed business distorts competition. This support does give true global companies a better-than-average

---

Practice Makes Perfect 3.1
Captive Customers

About 10 years ago, the practice of duty-free goods purchases for travel between EU member states had been abolished, except on the ferries that plied the Irish Sea. The ferry companies that operated routes between Ireland and Great Britain had managed to delay the abolishment of selling duty-free goods, in particular liquor, by endless appeals to their respective national governments, who in turn would appeal to the European powers. At last it looked as if the appeal road was exhausted, and duty-free would have to be ditched on these routes as well. In a last desperate attempt, the ferry companies employed a renowned consultancy that researched and subsequently "proved" in an extensive report that sales would decrease by at least 20%, and jobs would be lost for sure. In a lavish presentation attended by senior government, EU officials, the press, and other selected guests, these sad facts were highlighted and presented dramatically in colorful slides and a comprehensive, well-researched report. With the presentation complete, question time followed. One of the honorable invited guests, the CEO of one of the largest Irish retailers jumped up and said, "You mean to tell me that you have a captive client base for up to four hours, and you can't sell them anything?"

---

chance of survival, even if they have messed up considerably. However, in the longer term they often do not survive in their current form, as obviously something was quite substantially wrong. Current management is seldom the natural choice to right the wrongs and introduce significant change! In the writer's opinion, neither is government, but that's another story.

Naturally, all the above is very dependent on the type of products one deals in. Some products are more recession-proof then others. For example, video games might suffer minimally or not at all, while traditional white goods suffer considerably.

Be Always Attentive to a Lucky Break

And then there are always the examples of companies that hit the jackpot in a recession. A novel and unique one was recently (February 2009) given some media coverage in the United States, namely, a shrink-wrap business in Texas. Never having been associated with the building industry, this particular entrepreneur suddenly found his shrink-wrap services in demand to protect half-finished structures on building sites that were abandoned until demand picked up once more. His customary monthly sales of $150,000 shot up to $1.2 million in a matter of months. But, as we all know, these are exceptions that prove the rule—very nice for the benefit of the unsuspecting entrepreneur, but of no particular use in general to the rest of us. Unless of course you own a shrink-wrap business in upstate New York and can start marketing the same idea.

Advice for all companies large and small is quite simply, it never hurts to be on the lookout and to be open for unsuspected possibilities that might present themselves for a totally different application of your products or services. You will soon pick up the new market dynamics. Just be thankful for the initial lucky wild card that you were dealt, and keep it away from your competitors for as long as possible. Sometimes a wonderful world of new opportunities opens up to those who are alert and not scared to venture into the unknown.

What is important to retain from the above considerations is this: Your company's position in the spectrum of global-to-strictly-local will play a major part in its chances of survival during major market upheavals. A downturn always leads to considerable market readjustments, so concentrate on managing the business *now,* but keep an eye on major trends. In other words, and this is *lesson 1: relearn the parameters of your specific macroenvironment in order to "protect and continue to serve," to paraphrase a well-known police motto.*

THE CHEAPEST MARKETING TOOLS ON HAND

It's almost an "own goal" to make the statement that your business revolves around the happiness of its customers. This simple statement hides a multitude of possibilities and pitfalls that could make or break you in difficult economic times. With you and your competitors clamoring for business, it's very easy to lose customers, but it's much more difficult to acquire new ones, let alone entice the ones that stopped being customers to come back. So the brutal but simple logic is, try to not lose customers in the first place!

Also it's a well-known fact that it is a lot cheaper to retain a customer than to acquire a new one. Customer acquisition is a pretty expensive business and is beaten hands down in the cost stakes by customer retention. So, keep customers happy and coming back; there's nothing more to it really. These two well-known principles should be stamped on the foreheads of all your employees after you have stamped them on your own forehead. Set the example, remember? It's not complicated or involved, just very straightforward and unsophisticated. It's not even difficult to understand or complicated to introduce. Perhaps that's why these principles aren't practiced most of the time. It all sounds too simple! And that's where the real sting lies: *simple things are often very hard to apply consistently and continuously.* If all the statements that were thrown around by large and not-so-large companies about how they care for their customers were really practiced, there wouldn't be a disgruntled customer around, or not for long anyway.

A fine example of "keep them happy and coming" was presented many years ago by an acquaintance of mine. To me, he was the ultimate car salesman. Among other tools in his extensive customer care repertoire was this simple but highly effective system. Anyone who ever bought a car from him received a birthday card from that day forward. Every day of the year this salesman spent at least an hour or so on this activity. He had an extremely loyal, one could even say personal, customer base. When he left his employer, a well-known car dealership, and rejoined a different one, at least 60% of his customer base changed their brand allegiance too! By the way, this was in the good old days, with no computers, but only his personal card file system of all his past sales, organized by date of birth! The one thing that this fellow did superbly well was to put a bit of effort into staying in touch with his customers.

Keeping in touch nowadays is often confused with bombarding people with general mailings or e-mails. That's where smaller companies should have a big advantage. They often give up this advantage unwittingly by applying a level of sophistication practiced by their very large counterparts. Just because it's possible and relatively easy and cheap, that doesn't mean it's effective! A personalized note is worth a million impersonal emails. *Thus, cheap marketing tool number one is, be as personal as you can in your dealings and correspondence with customers.*

The Two-Faced Organization

In every organization, the sales force is well aware of the fact that its livelihood depends on its customers—one would hope so anyway; otherwise all would be lost! Unfortunately and frequently enough, that's where it stops. If as a customer you are confronted with office sales staff, dispatch, service, complaints, and so forth, you often get a totally different approach. It's almost as if these employees work for a different organization. Don't think that this applies only to very large organizations with masses of employees. Their problem is often that they haven't enough customer services staff to answer calls promptly, so most of us, customers I mean, have spent many minutes listening to that wonderful message "please hold; your call is important to us." In my travels and on many turnaround assignments I've come across the "one organization in two modes" for companies as small as 50 employees.

I've spent countless hours in medium-sized organizations explaining to all concerned that everyone's salary was dependent on that mysterious but oh-so-real concept of "our customers." I wanted to make sure that everyone adopted the principle of "Do what you promised the customer you would do." This means phoning her if necessary before the promised deadline to let her know that you haven't quite gotten to the bottom of her problem yet, but that you are on the case. These and many more simple, straightforward techniques, that one could refer to almost as basic courtesy, cost nothing, but can make the difference between customer happiness and never again! *Cheap marketing tool number two is teach all employees that customers are the one and only reason for the company's continued existence and their next paycheck. Number three follows immediately: as always, do what you promised the customer you would do!*

Listen to Customers

Another very unpretentious but frequently poorly practiced technique is just straightforward listening. In a world where almost everything is geared toward instant gratification and instant achievement, instant understanding seems to have crept in as well. We read only headlines and perhaps the odd bullet point, and form opinions on these very general and sometimes even misleading, but neatly packaged, bits of data. But remember, it's only data and not necessarily the whole story. You have only one chance during a telephone conversation or an e-mail reply to get the ultimate reward for good customer care, a happy customer, so take your time! The difference between considering a customer call an interruption and seeing it as an opportunity cannot be measured, but these two attitudes are a world apart. It will greatly influence the perception that customers will form of your organization. Of course it's always inconvenient, and it often is an interruption, but the customer is the *only* real reason for your own employment or your business! Thus, concentrate. Give the customer all the time she needs, by listening actively or reading carefully, and finding out exactly why she is e-mailing or phoning you. Actively listening or reading means postponing your conclusion until you know the full story! It's not a hit-the-buzzer contest with a quick right or wrong decision; it's a testing-understanding exercise with customer retention as the ultimate prize![4] There is no instant gratification or instant conclusion, just the knowledge that you have heard what the customer was really requesting or complained about, or sometimes even what the customer was happy about, and what's more, you fully understood her point of view. *Thus, cheap marketing tool number four is, always listen attentively to customers, and frequently practice testing understanding.*

Guerrilla and Ambush Marketing

An unconventional system of promotions, initially developed for direct consumer marketing for smaller companies, is *guerrilla marketing*. The term was coined by Jay Conrad Levinson in 1983, and the technique involves unusual approaches with minimal resources to get maximum results.[5] The three basic ingredients are time, energy, and imagination. Any form of publicity is allowed, but when such publicity approaches borderline acceptability, the technique is often referred to as *ambush marketing*. It is a questionable and sometimes even illegal practice. If you have really creative people on your staff, have the right consumer product, and stay within the bounds of the law, you can certainly get a fair bit of publicity for relatively little expense. Being able to maintain such an approach depends on whether you can produce a continuous stream of new ideas with different stunts. The term *guerrilla marketing* has also been hijacked to describe nontraditional ways of marketing, such as viral marketing through social networks, buzz marketing through word of mouth, undercover marketing through subtle product placements, and many more techniques. Large companies have started to use the technique as well, probably at high expense levels, using PR and marketing agencies, thereby somewhat corrupting the original idea.

Be Different

There are so many potential cheap marketing tools out there waiting to be implemented. Not all of them are applicable to each and every industry. But if you pick one and make it your own, you can start your organization or your department on the road to better customer retention. Look at what the competition does; look at totally different industries, and mold one item that really appeals to suit your own environment. Listen to your own staff, your customers, and other stakeholders. The possibilities are out there—just observe, analyze, and implement! Remember that the simpler it is, the more effective it will be, but also, the more difficult it will be to implement and to practice consistently and continually. *My cheap marketing tool number five is perhaps the most potent of them all: be different or even unique in one particular aspect that involves customers!*

In a following chapter even more attention will be paid to down-to-earth techniques to keep customers happy and coming back. But the five marketing tools described above can be summarized by saying, *get your customer service level to previously unmatched heights!* Do this not by talking about it, but by living it and, as managers, making sure that all your staff, including yourself, practice it continually and then actually start to enjoy

Practice Makes Perfect 3.2
The Color of Money

Quite some time ago, during one of my store visits while employed by a large retail chain, I observed, unnoticed, I might add, the following demonstration of basic customer service by the store manager. There had been some difficulties in that particular store with white members of staff treating customers of a different ethnic background with some contempt. After having explained in some colorful language that he was sick and tired of this, the store manager hit the enter key of the cash register, took out a "20," and asked his audience of three offenders, "which customer did this come from?" His answer was a stony silence. Then he said, "As long as I'm manager in this store, we will treat each and every customer as if she were personally paying our wages."

doing it. That is what will happen: you will enjoy dealing with customers because doing so is your organization's prime mission. Customer service is a way of life and not an interruption of the professed importance of office routines such as management meetings, internal conversations, coffee, and lunch breaks.

Online Businesses

Now I can hear some of you ask *but what about online businesses?* To my mind, an online business presents the ultimate test of giving the consumer what he wants by explaining what he is going to buy by means of video clips, pictures, and text. So, in a sense it's the same as a brick-and-mortar business. The primary difference is that with an online business, one has to anticipate common questions based on detailed know-how, expertise, and experience. The person running the online business must provide enough information for a buying decision to be made. This highlights the reason why certain products lend themselves better to online businesses than others. But don't come to that conclusion too hastily for your own products. Online business experts will keep on surprising us with more and more possibilities for buying online. This is an area that is still very much up for grabs, but if your product is introduced correctly, and your Web site is user friendly, you have a very potent and relatively cheap and efficient addition to more traditional marketing and selling methods. The emphasis here is most definitely on user friendly.

Basics Don't Cost Money

Any number of marketing experts will tell you that, particularly in a downturn, you should increase your marketing expenditure. Previous recessions are often cited, with accounts of how and when companies recovered. In general, companies who maintained aggressive marketing strategies during the downturn came out better than companies who cut marketing expenditure. So the conventional wisdom is to have the courage to increase marketing in the face of declining sales. These are wise words by experts and consultants, and most likely they are not wrong, either. But experts and consultants have no worries about your cash flow, out-of-balance expenditures, swollen staffing levels, and decrepit customer-care practices. These day-to-day essentials are your major concern, and they keep you awake at night! Instinctively we all know that in a prolonged downturn, looking after your existing customers and getting the ripple effect of effective customer service is excellent value for little or no cost at all. It's really quite simple, but it requires determination and attention to detail. It's much easier to hide behind an expensive marketing campaign to increase awareness of your products! That's why many preach, but few really practice, the really cheap marketing tools. And thus the cheapest of cheap opportunities, and *lesson 2 is to get genuine simple customer services right, and your marketing will be second to none!*

RUNNING A BUSINESS IS A TEAM SPORT

Let's continue our quest for beating the odds by relearning some home truth about managing people. Organizations are about people, and your job as a manager is, first and foremost, to get the most out of your people. A group of people trying to achieve an objective is referred to as a team. The team must be greater than its individual parts, and hence the output of a team must be much greater than single, uncoordinated outputs. When management greed becomes predominant, teamwork suffers, and negative motivation is the result. So it's up to management to reintroduce the concept of "business is a team sport, and what we are looking for are team players." Nothing world-shocking about this, but the concept will succeed only if an example is set. From the very start, it must be made quite clear that you, as a manager, are a team player as well. If you don't make this clear by example, take your chances. If you do lead by example in this area, you will notice a marked shift in commitment on the part of employees. The team is the ultimate vehicle of sustainable and enduring success in management and thus in business as well. When all is said and done, people enjoy being part of a team and reaping the success of the team, even if success at the moment just means survival of the business! This team concept might be particularly challenging for the Net Geners and some latter-day knowledge workers. Not really being used to playing on a team, they will find the transition from working alone and gaining personal satisfaction to being part of a team with a common goal particularly challenging, but also rewarding in the extreme—even more so if the individual tasks for each team member are well defined and challenging by themselves.

Team Basics

After a prolonged boom period and a mind-set focused on individual success and reward, the realization that "me the star" is fallible can be difficult to swallow. After all, when boom turns to bust, it's far too painful to

---

Practice Makes Perfect 3.3
We Are All in This Together

During a tough period for this particular multinational, a subsidiary in country Z was instructed, among other measures, to reduce the benefit of private car use for those members of staff who had the privilege of driving a company vehicle. In essence this reduction entailed that all private travel, including between home and office, had to be paid for by the staff member. In this particular country, full car benefits were an important part of senior staff remuneration practices. All the cost savings, including this change in car benefits, were presented at the subsidiary's head office in a formal session by the international vice president of finance, who had flown over for the occasion. While the VP explained the new car rules, he made quite a point to the local general manager that he (the general manager) was "obviously" exempted from this cost-saving measure. The local general manager himself was entitled to a vehicle with a driver at all times. The general manager did not bat an eyelid during this presentation. However, we soon noticed that after this unhappy event, he started coming to the office in what was described by one of my staff as a "clapped out" Volkswagen Beetle. Although we expected him to comment at one stage or other, he never mentioned his Beetle to anybody. We didn't dare bring up the subject! Soon afterward we heard that the driver of the general manager's car was required to drive him only from the office to appointments and back to the office, but that for home-office-home travel, "our" general manager used his own Beetle at all times.

---

take the overall blame all by yourself. The business world role models have been "winner-take-all" successful business leaders who invariably failed to apportion their success. The expression, "It's all thanks to my team" was forgotten and replaced by, "Even if I say so myself, I'm really pretty good." There were many instances where CEOs got paid 500 times as much as an average worker in the same company. This ratio went up tenfold over a period of less than 20 years. Difficult to explain to "team mates" who earn but a fraction of that, but are reminded frequently that "we are all on the same team." If we couple to this the predominant orientation in the past 10 years toward self-fulfillment, it's not surprising that the one composite management skill that really "lost out" in the latest boom was the skill to lead a team and to be a player on a team, with a common goal. After all, most managers would lead a team themselves and be part of another, often superior team as well.

Some time ago, Dr. Meredith Belbin described situations in which teams composed of "high flyers"—he called them Apollo Teams—performed very poorly compared with teams composed of more mediocre individuals. He called this failure the "Apollo Syndrome" and analyzed the poor performance, tracing it back to four main failings, namely,

(a) Apollo Teams spent excessive time in abortive or destructive debate, trying to persuade other team members to adopt their own views, and demonstrating a flair for spotting weaknesses in others' arguments.
(b) They had difficulties in their decision making, with little coherence in the decisions reached.
(c) Team members tended to act along their own favorite lines without taking account of what fellow members were doing, and the team proved difficult to manage.
(d) In some instances, teams recognized what was happening, but overcompensated, that is, they avoided confrontation, which also led to problems in decision making.[6, 7, 8]

Not every modern-day worker is a high flyer, but a well-developed sense of "me the brand" will compensate well enough for the Apollo Syndrome to infiltrate even run-of-the-mill teams and situations. Just when more and more social skills are required to function in and manage teams, more and more individuals are unfamiliar with the dynamics and interactions that make or break a team. Internet, Facebook, and "LinkedIn" activities, and blogging and computer games are no real substitute for teamwork and team leadership!

Specialized Knowledge Not an End in Itself

As most work becomes more and more specialized, teams, rather than the individual worker, will become the actual work unit[9]. This in itself is nothing new. Very few people could work effectively by themselves in the past. It just so happens that our focus on individual achievements and the concentration on technical knowledge transfer has made us forget that teams are required to effect the desired output. The most complex of teams that was touted often and could serve as a model for up-to-date teams, composed of modern-day workers, is the symphony orchestra. In an orchestra, each instrument section or specialized team, such as violins, flutes, trumpets, and so forth, performs its task, A flute player probably could not play the violin, and vice versa. However, together, under the direction of a conductor, they would achieve as a larger team. The conductor makes the various specialized units perform in harmony and produce the required output. What most modern-day workers will have to learn is to switch from one kind of team to another, that is, to integrate themselves into a team, what to expect of a team and, of course, what to contribute to a team. All of these are social skills that are no longer taught as a matter of course.

Team Management Skills

From the management point of view, it will become increasingly important to develop team-management skills. In other words, how can one make all the specialized knowledge productive? To again use the analogy of the orchestra, the task of the chief violinist is to make the violins perform in unison, this being a team of the same skills; the task of the conductor is to make all these specialized teams produce beautiful music. For the individual violin player, this means that he or she is part of two teams, the violin section and the orchestra. And, you will understand, the management skills needed to lead the violin section and the orchestra are quite different. Both are management tasks, but they are quite different in their output requirements. Thus, depending on the composition of the team and its desired output, different technical skills are required in combination with social skills. It is the latter skill that is frequently ignored in favor of technical know-how. Too often, management is still considered to be a bundle of techniques, such as budgeting, organizational development, marketing, and so forth, whereas the ultimate management skill, namely, to make a team productive, is still very much a social skill. The essence of civil engineering is not reinforced concrete technology, the essence of accounting is not the debtor ledger, and also the essence of management is not budget technique or marketing know-how.

Management is first and foremost a social function, and, particularly in its practice, it is much better defined as an art than a science.

Soft Skill Indeed!

And now for the dichotomy: managing a team might be called an art or a soft skill, but it requires a tough and discriminating attitude that can hold its own ground, but that at the same time does not dominate a team. Effective team leaders in the research carried out by Belbin were suspicious and skeptical people who sought to impose some shape or pattern on group discussion, and on the outcome of group activities.[10] They focused attention on the setting of objectives and priorities, and on shaping the way team effort was applied. All this must sound quite daunting to the current (2009) generation of self-centered, biased managers, and for that matter, employees. But have no fear; this type of behavior can be learned over time by practice and application of some basic techniques. After all, the "me first" practice was learned and perfected over time as well. Individual character is not being tampered with; it is behavioral change that is required. How this behavioral change is effected is up to each and every organization. There are plenty of good practical courses that teach basic group-interaction techniques, and, particularly in large organizations, the practice of experienced mentors to young managers could be reinstated.

In my own experiences, older, let's say 55+, managers enjoy being actively involved in on-the-job training to pass on practical management skills. So, before you all rush out and employ batteries of consultants to contemplate and introduce changes, and get involved in a formal "change program," look at this matter from the sensible point of view. Most consultants have never managed anything in their lives, so don't involve them in something that requires above all—you guessed it—management. The primary concern of practicing managers should be the mobilizing of action among employees, rather than endlessly discussing how action can be achieved at high-level and no doubt very costly meetings. Actions, your own included, speak much louder than words. *Lesson 3 is to relearn the art of managing, and particularly of managing modern teams of often diverse and specialized team members.*

THE NET GENERS ARE PART OF THE TEAM LIKE EVERYONE ELSE

The current (2008–?) downturn must and probably still will have a major effect on the youngest part of the working age population, the Net Generation, or Net Geners, for short.[11] This is the generation that had until recently experienced only economic growth and a pretty high standard of living. They tend to be well educated, privileged, and used to instant gratification. They tend to have found work without too much trouble, and they were mostly not overly committed to their jobs. They were ready to resign if their jobs were not fulfilling and fun, with decent holidays and the opportunity to take long stretches off for charity work or travel. As the saying goes, "they don't live to work; they work to live." Their general attitude is focused on doing well, but having quite a bit of fun in the process.

Quite a few managers have complained that after a childhood of molly-coddling and praise, Net Geners demand far more frequent feedback and an overprecise set of objectives on the path to promotion, rather like the levels that must be completed in a video game.[12] They typify their parents as "slogging their guts out" and as having a lifestyle focused on work; that model is most definitely not to be copied or desired! In short, it's a generation that believes it can have it all, and is not embarrassed to demand a harmonious balance between work and life. In the workplace, this younger generation is often described as self-centered, lazy, and smug by their bosses and older colleagues. In contrast, they themselves feel that they are putting in quite substantial efforts.

With this background in mind, it's going to be some mission to make Net Geners understand that times have changed. In the working environment, their preference for a relationship orientation approach, based on caring and inspiration, will most likely be replaced by task orientation. Job hopping to find the ultimate position that satisfies their spiritual needs will be difficult if there are no jobs to hop to. And then of course there are the unfortunate Net Geners who have experienced or who are going to experience being laid off. No doubt, quite a few managers who were sick to death about nurturing Net Geners will be quite smug about that. At last the overly sensitive human resources fads that always blossom in years of plenty are being ditched in favor of more brutal command-and-control methods. So far the generalities![13]

Net Geners Segmented and Other Groups Added

In practice, Net Geners are not that easily pigeonholed. For starters, there are big cultural differences among them. Whereas in the Western World the above-sketched generation label might stick for the majority, there are plenty of highly talented Chinese and Indian Net Geners heading our way. Intellectually hungry, focused on work achievements and academic success, they will present quite a challenge to the local Western World variety of Net Gener. Just look at the number of high-achieving Asian women studying mathematics and science compared with the number of home-grown students in those fields.[14] Job markets are turning global too, and for those willing to travel, the sky is indeed the limit.

It's also quite true that people of all ages share some of the desires of the Net Geners, but, due to prevailing circumstances and custom, it was better not to voice them! Who wouldn't want a better life-work balance, naturally with a high standard of living thrown in! It's also been said that Generation X, the "me" generation, born between 1965 and 1982, reluctantly adopted the work practices of baby boomers born between 1946 and 1964, but are envious of the Net Geners. How awful—stuck between a rock and a hard place! Matters get more and more involved, and the boundaries get more and more blurred.

To make things even more complex, the Net Geners are by no means the largest group of employees in most companies. With declining birthrates in a lot of Western societies during the past 30 years or so, they could even be considered a minority! In quite a few countries, workers aged 55+ comprise a much larger population group. Older workers are purported to be easier to manage; they require "less stroking," don't need major up-skilling, and tend not to be particularly ambitious for their next role. They can also be natural coaches for other members of the team. Also, as hard times persist, older employees with smaller financial commitments, no more kids to support financially, reduced mortgages, and so forth, might even welcome being "forced" to work four days a week. And then we haven't even considered the knowledge workers of late and other social groupings who have been typified by social scientists, human resources professionals, and the like. Yes, sir, it's a real hodgepodge out there, and there is no easy, prescribed way to treat them all. This may perhaps be difficult to understand for managers who are highly skilled in the scientific stuff, but who find themselves on shaky ground when it comes to "soft" skills.

Everyone a Team Member

That's my point exactly! That's why this all-important part of a manager's task, would you believe it, management, can only be introduced, but not mastered, at business schools and other learning institutions. This is where real life exposure and coaching are required. As a manager you must take each and every one of your team members as a member of your team. A good start is to treat them the way you would like to be treated yourself. Each one will have strengths and weaknesses, good points, strong points, weak points and annoying habits, but it's up to you to mold them all into a team that performs a vital function as a department or as a company. That's the very essence of management. Find and combine individual capabilities and tasks to achieve the desired end result. Don't forget that every member of the team must have her own individual tasks as well, that must contribute to the overall objective. *Lesson 4 to be relearned is to forget employee and generation labels; just develop people so they contribute to—and respect—the team.*

It's All in the Detail

Another principle that needs to be rediscovered, dusted off, and practiced vigorously by the team leader and the team is embodied in that simple expression, "It's all in the detail." A famous slogan in the retail world to express the relative importance of business parameters is location, location, and location. In business in general it should read, detail, detail, and detail. In essence, and on a daily basis, business is about the detail. To come up with the grand ideas is wonderful and of course sometimes necessary to move the business ahead. But on a daily basis, business is all about the detail and making sure the detail is attended to. For managers to believe and act as if someone else will look after the detail is the biggest mistake one can make, particularly in difficult times. It's a plain, simple fact that no one will look after the detail unless you have made absolutely sure that someone does! Let me say it again: "No one will look after the detail unless you have made definitely and unquestionably sure that someone does." The detail is often the very difference between doing something particularly well and doing something badly.

Why do similar businesses with similar products get such a diversity of actual results? It's the detail! Why do some businesses fail and others survive in the same market with similar products? It's the detail. So start to practice the management of the detail, and make the difference.

What exactly is the detail? The detail is everything that happens in a company, including the little, apparently insignificant aspects. It covers everything from customer service to timekeeping, and a host of other matters. Where do you start? An obvious start is anything that has a direct impact on your customers, and then to start slowly incorporating the indirect influences. Once you have control of some of the detail, don't let it slip. Hold on to it and make sure it becomes habit. Then move on to other detail and repeat the process. Detail, detail, and detail again.

Follow Up on the Detail

Closely related to the emphasis on detail is the unquestionable importance of follow-up. If you ask someone to do something and never check up, the next time that particular someone might just decide to do it in his own good time, or not to do it at all. You, as the manager, obviously didn't

Practice Makes Perfect 3.4
Managing by Wandering Around

This particular example relates to a large financial department, 75 employees, in a subsidiary of a multinational in the 1980s. The department was a real shambles, not a good word was spoken about it, and it was up to me to try to put it right. After the previous manager, diagnosed as "burned out," left about a year before, a well-known international consultancy firm was taken on to sort things out. On my first day I was introduced to the senior partner of this firm, who proudly pointed to a large cupboard full of reports, diagrams, minutes of meetings, and so forth, and told me that "a lot of useful work had already been done." He was keen to agree to a comprehensive hand-over period of about three to four months. Unfortunately for him, I had agreed with my new boss that consultants and interim management was overkill. He had agreed because, to date, after about a year, there had been no noticeable improvement, only substantial fees.

The first two months I did nothing else than wander around and talk to everyone in the department on an almost daily basis. My own office was the place where I left my coat and briefcase in the morning. Apart from local accounting requirements, the head office in the United States was fed 95 financial reports on a tight monthly schedule. The department itself was spread over three buildings on an extensive site, and one of the sections had never been visited by the previous manager, or by the consultants for that matter! That's what the supervisor told me, anyway.

As the supervisors and staff members slowly warmed up and opened up to me, they told me that they had never been asked so many questions and given so much attention. The picture became clear. For the past five years or so, there had been numerous attempts to reengineer the department with continuous changes and attempts to "streamline" the local and international flow of information. Management was changed a number of times, supervisors were moved about, departmental groups were split, rejoined, split again, combined—you name it, and they had undergone it. Unfortunately no one had ever bothered to match up the changes with actual work requirements or asked the opinion of the supervisors. So what happened was that supervisors and senior staff members just carried on doing what they had always done, never mind where they were physically sitting or who within the department they reported to. It was a mishmash of employees and supervisors who had to spend countless wasted hours in visiting members of their "output team" situated in a renamed section in another building. By just regrouping everyone into output units, as they had been five years previously, the main problem was solved. We, the supervisors and I, then tackled some real efficiency issues and procedural changes. The department went from scar to star in six "easy" months.

---

care that much whether it was done or not! By following up you can show that you care, and, what's more, you can give the employee the feeling that what she did was important. Don't think that this works only for lower-level employees. Senior managers are employees too, and they are perhaps even more inclined to not take your requests too seriously if you don't follow up.

All the above doesn't let you off the hook. You as the manager, the person responsible, remember, must retain overall responsibility. For that reason alone it's important to make sure that all the detail is attended to, to your satisfaction. It's a concept that appears to have disappeared with the prevalent boom-time practice of rewards that are individually geared, but distributing the blame at the lowest level possible, introduced in Chapter 1. When did you last hear a senior government official or a captain of industry say, "I screwed up?" Nevertheless, all of us, as managers, will have to come to grips with this renewed sense of responsibility and face the fact that we can't only take credit for the boom years and success. Now we will have to show leadership, set the example, and be committed during tough times.

There is any number of management books written about the principles of delegation, the importance of stimulating and motivating employees, and various other soft, but if used honestly and with integrity, really not-so-soft management subjects. Management can be made very theoretical and extremely complex, but the bottom line is, if you pay attention to the detail, and follow up continuously, you will have achieved 90% of what management is all about. After that, it's all relatively easy to create a team spirit, particularly if you are passionate about the business yourself, can transmit your passion to team members, and don't shy away from setting the examples. *Lesson 5 must be that managing a team is about detail and setting the example.*

WHY ARE WE ACTUALLY DOING WHAT WE ARE DOING?

A downturn is a marvelous opportunity to examine what you are actually doing as a company. This is not a trick question, nor is it meant as a challenge to start thinking about mission or vision statements; it's merely a simple question who needs an answer, or perhaps it comprises simple questions that need many answers. There will be quite a few of you who will react by saying, "Of course we know what we are doing." But do you really? One of the consequences of a prolonged boom period is that products, activities, practices, and so forth, have crept in without too much scrutiny. There might even be business acquisitions that were never properly integrated, capital projects that were half completed, or that were completed, but never really utilized, new fresh ideas put on hold because "who needs change when all is going great?" We also see swollen staff departments that feed on each other, internal procedures that serve no purpose, and so on and so forth. Now is the time to address all of these wasteful habits and incomplete projects and either cut them out or make them work.

Bad Habits Need to Be Broken

It's always a good idea to start a what-are-we-doing-and-why exercise internally. First of all, starting internally should have no affect on your customers, who in general have little interest in your internal processes and on the functioning thereof, as long as they get what they want on time. Look particularly at purchasing practices, internal procedures and reporting, extracurricular activities, internal meetings, and so on. In my past experiences I've come across stationery supplies that could sustain all the printers of that particular organization, at current consumption, for at least two years. Shelves full of discontinued products, of which the last one was sold three years previously. Stealth overtime practices as a concession by management to accommodate people who travelled to and from work together. No longer queried overtime of one hour a day for all warehouse staff due to a ruling that had required a bit of overtime more than a year ago. Easy introduction of temporary workers who have since become part of the household. Accepted-as-normal Saturday morning overtime instituted for all twenty-five employees of an IT Department to catch up on additional work, and so on. It would really surprise me if you couldn't find at least five to ten substantial "internal malpractices" in your organization! Don't leave the termination of these practices to chance by issuing directives only, such as the infamous memo "from today all overtime needs the approval of the general manager." You will find that you might end up rejecting regular one-time requests for overtime, while the accepted and structural ones are continued as usual. Remember one of the previously discussed golden rules of management—make sure you attend to detail. In this case, the detail is to examine the payroll and perhaps the personnel files and to note where overtime has been created, who approved it, and who has regularly used overtime. Why am I harping about overtime? Personnel costs are more than likely your biggest expense. By eliminating lucrative (for employees) overtime habits, you can save a lot of money. How much do you think the

Even Bad Practice Makes Perfect 3.5
"Over and Over Time as Overtime"

There have been so many examples of overtime abuse in my own career as a troubleshooter that it's an area well worth exploring for substantial savings in labor costs before redundancies are considered.

Case I concerns a multinational. Quite a few office staff members were permitted to start early, two hours early, in fact, in order to beat the traffic. Of course leaving early was not on because, due to the time difference, the phones from head office in the United States were just warming up at 3 pm in the afternoon. Hence there were two hours overtime for nearly 30 employees every day! To top it all, no manager had ever started early to get some feel for what was happening during these "early bird catches the worm" sessions. When I got involved, I started coming in early too, much to the surprise of the early morning "coffee and newspaper" discussion groups. The clubs were disbanded, and substantial savings were made on overhead costs. Needless to say, output was not affected.

Case II played out in a large production plant. Production was on a 5-day, 24-hour schedule. Day 6 was used for maintenance and general cleaning, and day 7 was a day of rest, as it should be. No manager had ever queried the number of people who worked on a Saturday or had even been to the plant on a Saturday, I might add. I love irregular hours, so at the first opportunity I came in early on a Saturday and, to my surprise, so did all plant personnel, all 125 of them. What materialized is that about three years ago the maintenance staff had asked the then–production manager whether some factory workers could help in order for the maintenance staff to concentrate on technical issues. This was eventually extended to include general cleaning, a chore that was supposed to be part of daily activities, and that had required a few more employees. This had snowballed into a general request for volunteers to work on a Saturday. As Saturday overtime paid 1.75 times the normal rate, there was never a lack of volunteers!

Case III was set in an installation and service environment. Although there was supposed to be only one crew on standby, all five crews were allocated numerous small but insignificant tasks spread out sufficiently so that travel time was maximized. Crews didn't mind at 1.75 times the normal rate, but the main culprit here was the service manager who made the schedule and who had to come into the office "to liaise" with his crews, read the newspaper, and attend to his hobby, building a model steam engine, using the company's workshop and getting paid overtime in the process.

organization that discontinued "we have always done it" Saturday overtime for its whole IT department saved on the payroll?

On a lighter note, my personal favorite habit breaker is the office supply salesman, who calls in once a week, brings flowers for the receptionist, or a box of cigars for the bookkeeper from time to time, and knows more about your organization than you think! Tell him to come only once a month; if you need something urgent between calls, you'll call him and order it. Then put someone in charge of reviewing purchases before they are actually made. Now some of you might say sarcastically, "Yeah, no doubt stationery is going to save the day." Let me enlighten you: I've come across consumption of ink cartridges in small companies that would make a printing company frown. But much more importantly, realize that it is also an attitude change we are after. All employees need to be shocked back to reality and get out of bad habits. Remember *lesson 6: it's all in the detail.*

Costs-Benefits Need to Be Examined

Start with having a good look at your product portfolio. Each product should be examined as to its contribution to your bottom line. If you have an extensive product portfolio, this will take some time. If you only have one or a few products or services, have a good look at the components. The result of this exercise should be that you continue or discontinue, make or buy, watch carefully for a while, and so forth. Now do yourself a favor and don't skip those accepted norms of the product cost picture, such as the allocation keys of overhead costs, contribution to head office costs, and all the other indirect costs that nowadays often comprise a much larger part of total product cost than direct manufacturing or purchase costs. That's where a good look at your staff departments comes in as well. What actually is their contribution and cost? Was the new MRP system that was introduced not supposed to reduce the staff in the logistics department by 20%? So why has there been a staff increase of 25%?

Questions, questions, and more questions that need to be asked and answered. Don't take no for an answer—just keep on asking, and make sure the detail is examined and attended to! I have done these exercises time and time again for companies in considerable difficulties, and the uncontrolled and never-queried costs that come to the fore are quite enlightening, if not frightening. One example of what surfaced was a product still manufactured for a very good client, that required major retooling in the factory, but that could be purchased from a small engineering shop for half the price, including the additional quality control measures that had to be taken. Or, considerable marketing expenses for a line of products that was well into the decline phase because the budget once allocated gave the respective account manager the freedom to spend. And a technical service department in a factory that had spare parts in its stockroom for secondary machinery to cater to more than one major catastrophe. By the way, the two suppliers of these parts guaranteed a twelve-hour turnaround, with installation thrown in. Just think of the implications for the cash flow of these accepted norms. In times of trouble, there are no accepted norms—only questions that need to be answered!

When Is the Benefit Due?

Capital projects and recently acquired companies are fertile grounds for cost-saving exercises. They tend to be trickier, but if you start looking at them now, you reap the benefits sooner rather than later. In particular I mean major ticket items, such as that recent acquisition of that oh-so-attractive company that would fit ever so snugly in your product portfolio. Or that ailing company that was bought because you, and only you, could bring it back to life, and so on and so forth. If there's one thing that I've learned in all my years as a troubleshooter, it is that mergers and acquisitions are an active minefield for all direct participants, and a beautiful rose garden for consultants. Whether it made sense or not is no longer of great interest, but how to deal with it today is of great urgency. Frequently, a downturn is not the right time for a quick sale to solve what has become a real problem and drain on the cash flow. On the positive side, the acquired company's management and employees, often reluctant players in your takeover game, are more pliable to adopt your "superior" methods and procedures and to cooperate more willingly in areas of common interest, such as supply contracts, sharing know-how, sales efforts, and so forth. So if your organization still believes in the acquisition, now is the time to seriously address all the integrating issues to get the one-plus-one-equals-three desired outcome on the road.[15]

Capital projects comprise another major ticket item that needs to be evaluated quickly as to their contribution to getting through the rough times. That new factory that is supposed to go onstream in six months, that new computer system that will streamline your data-processing requirements, the replacement machinery that the factory manager has had his eye on for some time, and that has been ordered, and so forth. Make quick evaluations and decisions. It's no good having the new plant delivered in three months while your cash flow is a mere trickle of its gushing past. These are tough decisions, but survival today goes before what is required tomorrow. The point has already been made that lovely theories and research about how much more difficult it is to compete in the future if you cut these costs now are probably not wrong.

But remember, all these articles are written by consultants and theorists who don't sleep an hour less because your cash flow is under real threat. The rule is very simple: *Survive today so you can still be in the fight tomorrow.*

The last major ticket item concerned with "what we are doing today" must be the employment of consultants during difficult times. Here again the accepted dictum is not necessarily the right one. There were no doubt good reasons why you employed them, so now let there be outstanding reasons why you keep them on. All projects can be postponed if cash flow dictates it. What's more, your and your team's complete attention are required to run the business as effectively as possible in order to survive. Unless you know that the short-term benefits are real, just discontinue consultant services, or you will discover to your detriment that your organization is subsidizing the consultant's survival.

Real Trouble

All the above deliberations pale compared to what needs to be done as a matter of urgency if your sales collapse due to the severity of a downturn.[16] One thing is for certain: if you don't see sales recover in the short-to-medium term, you'd better do something drastic to bring your costs back into line with your sales. Plant closures, major staff layoffs, heavy discounts on manufactured but unsold stock, and so forth, are all measures that need to be applied in order to retain some sense of balance and to retain some form of cash flow. Your competitors are probably in the same boat or sending out "maydays" from their own sinking vessels. This type of doomsday scenario attracts government protection for very large potential victims; pity the remainder, who will just have to fend for themselves! Nevertheless, *to relearn what you are doing and then do it as effectively as possible remains very valid as lesson 7.*

Relearn Lessons Summarized

1. Protect and continue to serve in a winner-take-all environment.
2. Use the cheap marketing tools, and your customer service will be second to none!
3. Master the art of managing teams composed of diverse and specialized team members.
4. Forget employee and generation labels; just develop people so they contribute to and respect the team.
5. Managing a team is about the detail and setting the example.
6. It's all in the *detail*.
7. What is it that we should be doing?

CHAPTER 4

FOCUS ON THE BASICS AND WHAT CAN BE CONTROLLED

A pessimist sees the difficulty in every opportunity; an optimist sees the opportunity in every difficulty.

—*Winston Churchill (1874–1965)*

WHAT DO WE DO REALLY WELL, AND WHERE ARE WE MOST VULNERABLE?

There is one positive notion that you should remind yourself of time and time again in a downturn, namely, we must be doing something right because we are still here. By itself that is a meaningless observation, but the underlying purpose is to force you to consider what has made you successful to date. A good place to start to find the answer to this question must be with your customers. As long as a business has customers, there is a reason for its existence. Whether it is a viable existence or not is another question that begs for an answer, but, at least, for the moment, there are some people or businesses that still trade with you. Let's find out why they do. Perhaps we can improve ourselves on what appeals to our existing customers to make sure they stick with us. Perhaps in the process we can gain some new customers. Now before you rush out, compile a questionnaire, distribute it to your customers, get the questionnaires filled in, and analyze the results, take a moment to reflect.

Customers Decide!

You want to find out from your customers what they like and perhaps what they dislike about your products or your company. It can't possibly be a quick snapshot, but it should be a continuous stream of snapshots starting today! Nowadays there are many direct and indirect ways of monitoring how customers react to your products. Use all those that are available to

---

Practice Makes Perfect 4.1
What's Really Happening Out There

In order to get a feel for what's really happening out there, I've certainly spent a lot of time visiting customers with sales personnel. But what I've also done on various occasions is to travel with delivery vans, as part of the crew, to get a feel for what's happening at the "back door" of a receiving client organization. This works particularly well if your products go into the manufacturing process of your customer. Not only do you pick up on how your products are received and treated, but you also learn how they are stored and handled. It's all useful for future changes in packaging, transport, and so forth. It also gives you an opportunity to talk informally to delivery crews in their cabs (their offices), and not in your own. They are away from the company most of the time, and they need to feel part of the team too. After all, you can shower all the attention you want on your product, but if delivery stinks, you spoil it all!

In one instance in the 1990s, I noted that, although our products had to be packaged as if they were going to live in a box for quite some time, all packaging was ripped off before it went to the customer's storage area! The way I found that out was that I was on the dock when the receiving supervisor said, "here comes another load of unnecessary work." We got our salespeople to talk to their production people—and we saved over 60% on packaging! A substantial amount of that saving was passed on to the customer.

In a different setting I experienced that a particular route as set by the supervisor, GPS and "fastest route," you know, had a few really nasty obstacles and delays for the drivers. The drivers had suggested alternative routes, but the supervisor was one of those "Me Boss; You Do What I Tell You" types. The supervisor himself had never even been on a route. Working with the supervisor for some time, I slowly got him to listen to his own staff and to adopt some of their suggestions. He was a much better supervisor for it! *Remember, listen to the people who do their specific part of the overall mission every day, and you might learn something!*

---

you, including new ones, such as monitoring chat sites, consumer protection Web sites, trade magazines, you name it. Discuss the results with your staff. Formal well-proven methods can be used as well, such as recording complaints, logging late deliveries, keeping track of damaged or broken on-arrival complaints, tracking the number of telephone calls to customer service, listing types of complaints, and so on. Don't start off by saying, "It's very difficult to do that for our products," or "that wouldn't work in our industry." I've heard that hundreds of times, but in the end there was always a way to find out what was going down well with customers and what was a real bone of contention.

Not so long ago I purchased a handheld rechargeable gadget via an e-store. All went well until the battery had to be recharged for the third time. Somehow or other the internal battery didn't hold its charge at all. I sent the whole thing back to the manufacturer with a short note. A few weeks later I got a brand-new one from them with a letter of apology. Unfortunately the second one appeared to have similar problems. After a couple of weeks the internal battery refused to do its job. Now I took the trouble to start a bit of a search on the Web. Lo and behold, I came across quite a few customer product reviews that indicated problems similar to what I had encountered. The general consensus was, it's a lovely gadget; it's a pity about the internal battery; I won't buy again! Now, about a year later, the same complaints persist. Is nobody out there listening? Don't let that happen to your company! Stay very close to your customers, and really find out what they like and dislike about you. Then find ways and means to improve!

Vital Internal Support

It is in this area where a lot of companies fall down. Product fine, sales force committed, after-sales sucks, account staff downright rude! Sales force running around to apologize for the company, gets little backing from the office: "far too busy, you know"; everyone wonders why clients don't come back: "we have such good products."

It's the task of management to make sure that, when the sale is made, the service begins! Make it happen in your business! If your sales force is selling what is in your product portfolio; the follow-on will decide ultimate success. I'm a really reluctant grocery shopper at the best of times, so home delivery seemed just the thing for me. I've tried it twice from the same company, and both times there was something wrong. Great Web site, exciting bargains, on-time delivery—but items missing on both occasions, delivered afterward—an inconvenience to me. So much for that! It's the total package that leads to customer satisfaction, and thus the whole organization, yes, all employees from cleaner to director, needs to be focused on the *big C*. There are many ways in which after-sales service can be improved that will lead to customers coming back. In a made-to-order production environment, I was on one of my regular field trips with the area sales manager when I asked a particular customer; "why do you order from us?" I knew that one of our competitors had a plant much closer to them. Also transport costs were not insignificant, and that fact was not really working in our favor. His simple answer was, "You folks always deliver when you promise; we never have to chase you down."

After-sales service is a wonderful opportunity to find out whether customers are happy. Teach the technicians to ask open questions, such as, "Are you happy with it?" And to reinforce with remarks, such as, "This unit gives little trouble. It just goes and goes." Let them give feedback, and digest it with all other information. Encourage them to think of themselves as being on the front line of customer contact. If possible let them interface with the sales force frequently.

Credit control is an area where most companies don't even think about customer service any more. Nevertheless, it can be made an integral part of the total service experience if company representatives are polite but firm, making sure that there were no hiccups in what went before. Let staff be proactive, and first find out whether there are any possible reasons why payment has not been made. This approach allows for a much more confident phone call, such as, "I've checked with sales and dispatch, and they are not aware of any problems. So I wonder why payment has not been made." Even if the contact is between accounting staff from both parties, a good rapport between them will often result in information about when payment is going to be made. Focus all staff on the Big C; it doesn't cost anything bar perhaps short weekly in-house sessions to give them tips and to share experiences. All employees must start understanding that customers are the only reason why they are employed. So teach them, involve them, and consult them. *Your organization has nothing to lose but a client!*

So What Are We Really Good At?

With the benefit of some of the methods and techniques described above, ask the question again, what are we really good at? Now try to be even better at it. For a lot of companies that supply products that are the same or very similar to those of their competitors, the answer will probably lie in quite a few small things that make customers come back or, alternatively, that cause them to say "never again." So make sure the unsung heroes of dispatch, delivery, service, accounts, and so forth, get to hear the good news as well as the bad. If something gets messed up, they always hear about it, so it will make a nice change to compliment them and spur them on to even greater efforts. Sessions that are held to discuss company performance including service levels and client feedback are an excellent way to motivate all employees to keep on focusing on the topic. It really reinforces the team feeling and spirit that you require to make everyone in the organization passionate about what you are doing. That is what team learning and performance are all about.

Your Achilles Heel

Particularly in a downturn, you might feel that your Achilles heel has been hit by so many arrows that you don't know any more which one to pull out first. But smart managers don't panic; they look bad news in the eye and find a way to deal with it. Just remember, the difference between good and bad is often not that great when it comes to a lot of things that can be improved in a company. Most of the practices described so far fall in this category. It's the "all in the detail" refrain once more. Nine out of ten areas that can be improved upon are related to customers, so the old adage "Your greatest strength is also your greatest weakness," still holds. That should come as no surprise any more! It also means that if you address customer issues, you are addressing most of the manageable vulnerabilities.

There is seldom one particular reason why a company sinks in a downturn. Not unlike small improvements, there were probably lots of wrong decisions in the past that led to the straw that broke the camel's back. Spectacular failures are not that common, but if they do occur they get a lot of publicity. That's what sticks in all our minds. But it soon emerges that the downfall was in the making for some time anyway, the demise was just very well camouflaged. So take it to heart, and start a process of incremental improvements. Your company has just as much chance of surviving as your direct competitors have and maybe an even better one. It all depends on what you start doing from today on, without looking back.

Cash flow problems probably rank very high on the list of vulnerabilities. That's why so much effort must be put into managing your cash flow.[1] It probably needs to be adjusted to new realities, such as a lower level of activity and consequently a lower level of expenditure. That might require some very tough decisions on the cost-cutting front, but when survival is at stake, these decisions will have to be made. Think them through, and then decide and implement effectively. The sooner you act, the sooner you can concentrate again on the more positive things, such as how to retain and get more customers!

CONCENTRATE ON THE BIG C

Everything that we do in a company is important. A well-run business is like a good orchestra, producing wonderful and enjoyable music. We have already discussed the importance of the orchestra performing as a well-tuned team.[2] However, if the orchestra does not attract any listeners whatsoever, all the practice, talents, and dedication of the musicians and their conductor are to no avail. The orchestra will play no more; it will cease to exist, and it will be relegated to the pages of history. An orchestra needs listeners, and, as a pure analogy, a business needs customers—the *big C,* as I call it. This comparison is well understood by the majority of employees; why then is it so difficult to make *everyone practice* this simple principle? The answer is just as simple: a lot of employees don't really care! And they don't care because you, as a manager, don't really care, or don't remind them on a regular basis of the big C focus. Your sales department—let's assume it is customer focused—is fighting two battles: one is to convince customers to do business with your company, and another is to convince the company that getting a customer to do business with you is a good thing! When times are not so good, it's absolutely critical to concentrate all efforts on customer retention.

Who Are Your Customers?

This battle between sales and the remainder of the organization is fought in part because a lot of businesses have not properly defined what really constitutes their big C. You can't be all things to everyone at all times. This notion leads again to the question, what are you really good at? Never mind what you would *like* to be good at. Just simply, what are you doing at present and doing well? This question needs to be answered urgently because one thing is for certain: the chances that you will hold onto an unhappy customer that you should not have served because of your own business's limitations are as great as failed bankers returning bonuses. So if you haven't already examined your business and defined the customers you want to serve, do this as a matter of urgency. It might initially reduce your product or service portfolio somewhat, but it should improve your service levels, increase employee commitment, and ultimately enhance customer satisfaction. It's a lot easier to explain to your own troops that customer care is everyone's concern if you don't ask them to fit square pegs into round holes; that is, provide only what you are capable of providing.

You can be inventive, but within your own capabilities; thus you should concentrate your efforts on what the organization can achieve. Do not be tempted by customer requests that are clearly beyond your present capabilities. They only divert you from your real strength. By the way, this has nothing to do with innovation. Innovation is a process that will add to your capabilities in a planned and structured manner. Doing something that your organization is not really capable of doing is asking for trouble. It is like selling ice cream in a hardware store, or selling hammers in an ice cream parlor. The spectacular collapse of the banking system is a striking example of losing track of one's accepted business model. For most industries, failure on this scale would have meant total destruction. Only the commitment of governments to defend their banking systems removed this threat for the big institutions anyway. So stick to the knitting, and learn to say no if the desired product is clearly beyond your organization's capabilities.

Naturally, if you are part of a made-to-order company, the involvement of every department during the acquisition phase is an absolute must. This is so particularly during a downturn when a lot of companies are looking for better value or cheaper suppliers. So don't be caught as the organization that satisfied everyone outstandingly, but in the process goes bust spectacularly. Your own survival is the issue here, not the survival of all those real and alleged customers.

The decision of who your customers are can be facilitated by particular groupings or segments that marketing experts have identified over the years. The latest general segmentation efforts, particularly tuned to a recession environment, have yielded another layer of customer segments that could be superimposed on your existing ones. This is further expounded upon in Appendix E. Whether this could be of benefit to your efforts to determine who the customers for your own business are, only you and your team can decide. Most of this research is focused on consumer marketing while business-to-business marketing is even more difficult to partition. Nevertheless, it never hurts to be aware of the latest theoretical consumer marketing efforts to segment "all of us" into even smaller bite-size groups.

Selling Is *Not* a Lesser Business Skill

There are a lot of latter-day, highly educated managers who seem to think that selling is one of the lesser business skills. Business schools in particular tend to totally ignore the simple yet brutal truth that

no sales = no customers = nothing to manage.

Hence, is it surprising that most MBA graduates find the art of selling somewhat beneath them? We already pointed out in Chapter 1 that very large companies tended to compensate for this and for other new recruits' deficiencies by on-the-job-training. But in many other organizations, graduate employees don't have that advantage. In addition, the way to the top often does not require an exposure to salesmanship. As a result, ambitious young managers persist in believing that an understanding of selling and the techniques involved are not really fundamental skills associated with senior management functions. A downturn is a fantastic opportunity to address this real and serious deficiency. Thus, make sure that younger managers are introduced to selling techniques and that they spend time "on the floor" or "on the road." It's a great life experience for them, and it also makes them come to grips with the biggest personal inhibitors of selling, namely the fear of failure and rejection. If that doesn't build character, I don't know what does!

Selling is no doubt very direct and very measurable, and so much of it is also putting your own ego on the line. Fortunately, it is seldom personal. Still, knowing that sales rejection is not personal does not make the rejection any easier. Personally, you will still feel annoyed, frustrated, or even angry. You never really get used to rejection. All you can do is accept it as part of the sales experience. Explain to your managers that one has to learn to accept rejection in sales, but you don't have to like it. You just have to cope with it and do it all over again tomorrow. Fear of failure and selling are also inextricably linked. But at the very core, fear of failure is probably one of the greatest positive motivators in selling and in business in general, for that matter. If you are afraid of failure, then you probably care enough about success as well.

Naturally, a belief in your own products and organization is very much critical to selling. Make sure that everyone who hits the road or the floor has come to grips with your products and is capable of talking about them passionately. Customers do pick up pretty smartly on sales people (or on junior managers in training, for that matter) who have a take-it-or-leave-it approach. Formal and on-the-job training, continuous reinforcement, feedback, and correction are essential ingredients to any sales effort.

Now Really Value Customers

Back again to what now has become *your big C.* There are many ways to increase overall awareness of the importance of customers to your organization. But before we go into some of these techniques, you as a manager must be prepared to set the example. Lead by example, a forgotten principle in individualistic boom times, needs to be resuscitated swiftly and consistently. How can you expect employees to take customer service seriously when you don't practice it yourself? Clearly you can really preach effectively only when you yourself believe with a real passion. So learn to love your customers. In other words, *if you want to add value for customers, you first need to value customers.* In every new assignment I have had in the past twenty years, I spent an inordinate amount of time in the field getting to know the sales force, how they dealt with customers, and, conversely, how customers dealt with them! I've travelled with salesmen, merchandisers, delivery vans, and service vans, and I've dealt with customer complaints. Through all of this I've learned one important lesson: the more seriously you yourself take customer service, the more seriously it is taken by your staff.[3] A well-known Dutch proverb states, *"Goed voorbeeld doet goed volgen."* Loosely, this translates to "A good example will be followed." So if you want to increase your organization's or your department's awareness of its customers, start with yourself!

Quite popular in the 1980s and 1990s were programs that endeavored to teach departments in large organizations the principles of "internal customers." Forget it! It just distracts from the one and only big C. Government departments, particularly in some countries in Northern Europe, have started to refer to citizens as "their customers." So you get the ridiculous situation in which you are a "customer" at the police station and, believe it or not, at the tax office. It's never going to work, because in general terms civil servants have no idea how to treat free-to-choose customers.[4] It's like the internal customer ploy: a captive, no-other-choice audience can never be compared with a commercial, vote-with-your-feet-and-wallet customer. One thing is for certain, though: the principle of "lead by example" is universal and equally applicable to all environments.

Practice Makes Perfect 4.2
Meet the Customer

During my time at a large retail company that employed about 15,000 people in 600 stores, the then–CEO instituted a simple rule to make everyone aware of "what we are all about." Namely, anyone at executive level had to spend a minimum of one Saturday a month in a store in a customer-contact function. No executive was exempted. The program was referred to as "Meet the Customer," or MTC for short. In order to comply with this rule, all executives had to pass the basic on-the-job-training programs for sales assistant and cashier, a total of twelve self-study modules rounded off by a test paper to demonstrate proficiency. Each executive could select the store where she would spend the Saturday, but at least four different stores had to be part of the yearly 12 practical Saturdays. The manager of the store where the executive spent her customer contact day had to certify, on the executive's MTC score card, that the executive was employed on the floor for a minimum of eight hours. The CEO himself took part in the program and never missed his 12 Saturdays. The program was so successful that it was extended, voluntarily I might add, to all head office staff. As an added benefit, this voluntary part of MTC was a great help to break down the barriers between "them" at the office and "us" in the field.

Teach Customer Service

When you yourself are truly committed to customer service, you can start teaching it to your staff. In a world where instant gratification and instant recognition are paramount, you will have to teach your staff to listen carefully to what a customer has to say. Now obviously, if a customer wants an orange pair of men's socks in size 9, there is little room for misunderstanding, don't you think? But a dedicated sock salesman will beg to differ. There are woolen socks, cotton socks, part cotton and part something else socks, bright orange, pale orange, and so on. This somewhat ludicrous example tries to illustrate that there is always need for testing understanding before you take action. That leads to another very important point, namely, teach everyone in your organization product knowledge. Set aside short periods twice a week, fifteen minutes tops, to teach all, and I mean *all,* employees what you are actually selling. Call these sessions what you like. I've called them PACE sessions in the past, but make them interesting and compulsory, and test for comprehension continually.[5] Vary the sessions by letting other managers and specialists lead some of them. Now I can hear the managers in multifaceted engineering works say, "That will never work for us; our products are far too complex." But that's exactly why it's so important. If you can't "lift out" the really important features of your products and explain them to everyone in the organization, you will fight a losing battle on the customer services front. Make your employees understand the basics and create product know-how, interest, awareness, and, above all, pride—yes, good old-fashioned pride in your business!

Teach Your Customers

Another area that must be explored is teaching your customers. Pharmaceutical companies are past masters at this, and they continually educate their indirect customers, the doctors who prescribe medicines, as to the benefits of their products. Not every product lends itself to a similar treatment, but don't dismiss the matter too easily either. Any opportunity to explain to customers what your products and services can do for them must be exploited in full. In the construction industry, I have used a company newsletter to bring that company's overall achievements and projects to customer attention. It was dressed up as an internal newsletter, but field managers were instructed to leave them lying around in as many places as possible. After about six months, we found that the newsletter was read by just about everyone on each and every construction site. During breaks, site personnel and visitors were always looking for something to read! Talk about cheap publicity.

Hold classes and how-to sessions on your products and services for your customers or their staff. Make these sessions free, and invite as many customers as possible. Record some of the sessions and send copies to some clients who couldn't make it. On a more modern note, let your younger employees use their network savvy to discuss your products and services on the Web. Help them to present your company's case effectively by being honest and making sure they keep you informed of what and how the discussions flow. Youngsters who are not happy about something can in particular do untold damage. Be on top of this by being aware of what is being discussed and

---

Practice Makes Perfect 4.3
Little Things Mean a Lot

Whether the large, made-to-order products came from us or from someone else was difficult to determine. The main ingredient was concrete, and apart from saying facetiously, "We can always smell our own concrete: it's the water you know," there was little difference between our products and the products of many a competitor. Naturally, in this type of industry, price is a major factor, but so are delivery, dimensional correctness, and quality of finish. We had been racking our brains as to what else we could do to differentiate our product without adding substantial costs, when the commercial director came up with a truly unusual suggestion. It all had to do with test certificates.

Every concrete mix requires the taking of test cubes at regular intervals. These test cubes are matured and then tested to destruction in order to prove concrete strength. The laboratory requirements for this type of test are rudimentary. Records need to be kept, and clients could ask for test certificates, which they seldom did. If they did ask for them, it was always at the end of a project in one mammoth file. Linking the concrete to the product was based on the time of the latest mix, the time the test cubes were taken, and the time of the pour.

The commercial director's idea was to send a test certificate with every completed product. The certificate would be printed on our custom-designed stationery with our logo displayed prominently, in a very appealing layout. It took awhile to design the certificate in such a way that it looked really attractive and was linked to the product production file. Then, thanks to modern software, it took just another press of the button. Our clients received this innovation with some praise, and what's more it instilled confidence by showing a proactive approach.

---

how it's being discussed.[6] Some research suggests that Net Geners place more emphasis on personal recommendations than on brands.[7] Use this to your advantage, and milk it as much as you can. Have an up-to-date customer mailing list and mail your customers new developments, offers, novelties, and so on and so forth. Seek responses, and develop methods to analyze reactions and to adjust your approach if required. Continually update your approach to incorporate previous findings. Use e-mail and printed matter, depending on your customer profile. See how others do it, amend their techniques to your own needs, and implement.

All of these matters fall into the "not expensive" category, but they do create brand awareness or brand loyalty. After all, your own company, regardless of size, is a "brand," too, for its customers. When we talk about "brand," we often think only of the world-famous brands, such as Mars, Coca Cola, Armani, Jeep, and so forth. But brand is just as important for Charlie's Café, for Pete the Plumber, and for Bert the Builder. It is just a matter of scale, but that should not really be an issue for the business itself; customer perception and perceived value must be the issue.

Thank Customers

Nothing is simpler in life than to say, "thank you for doing business with us." When times are tough, you have to do it more frequently! We all know that the first sentence in the operating instructions of any appliance ever bought, whether large or small, is "Dear Customer, thank you for buying . . ." Now amend this impersonal message to your own business environment. If you or one of your employees can think of a small twist, use it! It's all about differentiation and making it known that you really appreciate the support of your customers.

Keen salespeople and small business owners have long since practiced the art of phoning, or better still of visiting their clients, and thanking them for their order. In the process they find out a lot of things that could be of great interest to their organizations. People who are thanked for being customers love to talk. It's called post-purchase behavior in marketing jargon. Often customers open up a bit more, so you can preempt some of the issues that might come up with the next order, or issues that are going to be raised during installation or delivery. Don't forget that the purchasing manager who might be your customer will react in the same way as consumer customers. The title makes no difference. It's basic human behavior. Give someone attention in a nonthreatening, thankful way, and you "stroke" him or her into feeling even better about purchasing from you.

Create Value

There is a big difference between price and value. Every successful small retailer will tell you that he or she can't compete with major competitors on price, but can compete on value. What constitutes value is in the eye of the beholder, and that is exactly the opportunity for smaller companies to compete with much larger organizations in similar industries. Whether value is related to service, location, convenience, or quality doesn't really matter. Set yourself the task of finding at least five areas where you can be different from your competitors. Implement them, but don't sit on your

---

Practice Makes Perfect 4.4
If You Do the Crime, You Must Do the Time

It had been a long day with plenty of "opportunities," but perhaps that particular day there had been one too many of these. My assignment was in its first month, and that's always crunch time with plenty of surprises and can after can of the proverbial worms. The call came when I had put on my coat and was ready to leave the office. It was one of our customers, a purchasing manager from a company not yet known to me, who wanted to speak to the new "top man" because he had a complaint worthy of my attention. After taking about half an hour of his monologue, a quality issue that could be resolved quite easily, and with me trying to interrupt politely to assure him that all would be taken care of, I lost my cool. I tore into him and told him that this issue would be dealt with tomorrow by his usual contact person and slammed down the phone.

Driving home, I felt terribly guilty. Here I was preaching customer service to an organization that, in my opinion could do with a lot of it, and there I was setting a really classy example.

Next morning I went to the office, found out where this customer's office was, and set off. When I got to meet him a few hours later, I groveled and apologized profusely without any excuses. His voice, so grating to me on the phone, was not much better in real life, and he lectured me for well over an hour about past difficulties with us, his own difficulties, his company's difficulties, his private difficulties, and so on and so on. I just sat through it; listened politely, put a real zip on it, and this time kept my cool. It wasn't easy, I tell you!

We didn't lose his company's account, but I've never forgotten that it would have been a lot easier to "zip it" on the first call. "If you do the ..."

---

laurels. If you are successful, your competitors will quickly copy you, so try to keep ahead of or at least with the pack. Just look at retailers and see how quickly the super-saver pack, the economy pack, the 25%-free pack, the buy-five-get-one-free methods are copied by all and sundry. Personally, I'm a firm believer in getting the areas surrounding the actual product to higher levels. Such areas include store layout, trading hours convenient for your customers, attentiveness, installation, service, quality, and delivery. These measures tend to be more effective, and what's more, addictive, to customers.

Ask yourself the question, how is value created in our industry and in our company? Find the answers, and jump out of the downward cost-cutting spiral that is an inevitable consequence of competition in a downturn. Create value, but watch margins! It's oh-so-easy to improve all aspects of your product offerings, but then to be caught out by all those indirect value-adding costs that are accounted for in a different way. There's no point in adding value that ultimately leads to your own demise!

SAVINGS MUST BE FOUND

There is no doubt that a long spell of good times makes all of us easier spenders and perhaps even casual risk takers. Of course, companies that operate in very competitive markets are kept tighter than those in less-competitive markets, but, as we all know, everything in business life is relative too. I've seen too many companies in difficulties, even during good times, not to know that cost reductions can always be made, even by companies that feel they can't possibly make them. It's all a matter of going through your organization, or department, if you like, in a logical and systematic fashion. What you should try to achieve is a "zero tolerance to waste and unnecessary activities" mentality for all. Needless to say, you must start at the top. It's perhaps not where the biggest cost savers are to be found, but it sets the tone and, what's critical, the example. Recall that we are leading by example. After cancelling the director's luncheon before every weekly management meeting, closing down the director's and senior executives' dining room, reviewing your personal interest or hobby sponsorships, cancelling the next executive meeting at that expensive and exotic golf resort, and having reduced the company car pool appropriately, you can get down to the *real business* of trying to discover where savings can be made.[8] After these mostly symbolic cuts, you should also have the full attention of the organization. If you and your management team are prepared to suffer, you must be serious about achieving expenditure cuts. So use the executive example-setting to get the organization's attention.

Rethink, and If Required, Divest Your Product Portfolio

The second critical tier of the top approach is to examine your product portfolio and to see whether there are some real drains on your cash flow. There are bound to be products that contribute marginally, or that even cost money. It goes without saying that one needs to exercise care because cost reductions, coupled to revenue decreases, are notoriously difficult to examine because of the many interwoven activities. For example, you probably won't be in a position to reduce factory staffing levels by cutting out a few unprofitable lines. Always consult your sales force. Sometimes low-margin products are an integral part of the overall product portfolio. Nevertheless, at this stage you must evaluate, consider eliminating, decide whether to make or buy, or investigate other scenarios applicable to your company. By the way, divest or invest decisions should be a regular feature of all management team discussions. It requires a fair bit of homework to make these decisions. That's why time is of the essence. The sooner you find out what contributes and what doesn't, the earlier you can start earning your pay and make the right decisions to divest in some products.

Divesting the company of unprofitable activities is the most efficient and beneficial way to address the causes of diminishing performance. It doesn't come easy, and it requires a cool and logical approach, difficult in turbulent times, but it goes right to the heart of business survival. Evenly and democratically cutting costs across product lines or functional divisions is easy, but it smacks of fire-fighting or "finger-in-the-dike" behavior rather than addressing basic questions, such as where and how do we add value, does our business model requires a major rethink, how are we financed, and so forth. A downturn can mark a clean break with the past and force these decisions to be made. After all, scarce credit and reduced demand justify hard choices that were not required during the boom years. By concentrating on day-to-day operations, controlling your costs effectively, and reevaluating the allocation of your scarce resources to promising areas or products, you might just turn a downturn into an opportunity.

Set the Internal Savings Target

Set your management team and yourself the target that is required to achieve the correct balance between revenue and costs. Don't get involved in endless discussions. Any implementation delays will not be reflected in retrospect in your cash flow. The burn rate will continue unabated. The sooner you can put some water on it, the better it is. Very large organizations often dictate that every company, department, and unit needs to cut back by, for example, 20%. It's a rough method, but it will often have the desired effect. Whether it is always a wise approach depends on the circumstances. In smaller organizations, it is not an approach that I would suggest at all. Look carefully at current returns, weigh alternatives, and consider embryonic projects and developments. Don't forget that every manager will think that hers is the only department that has been well run and that she cannot possibly operate with fewer staff. If the savings target is set, presumably taking cognizance of the lower revenue figures, then you had better achieve it. You did not set it for nothing! A downturn means attending to today's problems and keeping a keen eye on the long term. The intermediate period tends to be totally unpredictable, so it's good-bye budget and sales forecast, and hello cost control and new opportunities.

Identify Internal Savings

There are various techniques that have been used in the past to identify cost reduction opportunities, including zero-based budgeting. It is not uncommon for organizations to base this year's budget on last year's, plus or minus an inflation correction. There are obvious advantages to such a quick and dirty approach, but these actions tend not to be associated with careful scrutiny. Zero-based budgeting, as the expression implies, starts with no reference and therefore all costs should be based only on the necessary activities that are required to achieve the revenue targets. It's a great idea, but probably far too cumbersome in practice. Somewhere in between lies the practical approach to seeking out cost reductions. This is where the total team comes in as well. Having shown by the top-down approach that you are serious in seeking cost reductions, you can appeal to all employees for suggestions. How you do this is a matter of preference.

In the past I have used shop floor talks, supervisor forums, small project teams, suggestion boxes, and so on. Just use the approaches that seem most appropriate in your own environment, but pursue them with a passion, while your management team concentrates on an overall examination of costs related to benefits. Do the examination properly, and don't be tempted by the so-called gut feeling. We all have gut feelings, but we tend to remember only when our gut feeling was right, and not when it was terribly wrong. That's human nature. So analyze, scrutinize, and examine, and then come to a decision with your management team. If it is a unanimous decision, so much the better, but if opinions are divided, you will have to earn your pay by making the decision.

Practice Makes Perfect 4.5
Using a Sledgehammer to Crack a Nut

The company had been burning cash steadily for the past couple of years. The owner, a devoted and very knowledgeable engineer, had only one thing in mind, how to get out gracefully. But gracefully is not easy to achieve when you are bleeding profusely. There were two main parts to the operation, centered around four pretty sophisticated machines. Two had been there since the beginning, five years previously. Let's refer to them as type A, and the other two were commissioned a few years later. Let's call them type B. Type B was much more advanced than type A, and it was a lot more versatile. There were about 120 employees in total. Only a nine-hour day shift was run. Cost control was very rudimentary.

After about two months in charge, I wasn't really any closer to finding out where substantial savings could be made. Sales were steady, our prices were competitive, and customers appeared to be happy. Then a thought struck me. Did the introduction of type B have an effect on the overall operation? On quick examination, it was suggested that the troubles had started after the two type Bs were commissioned. Some detailed analysis was called for. The financial controller and I started unraveling the operations in a major cost accounting exercise. What became clear was that everything associated with the type B machines was much more expensive. For one thing, set-up time for type B was more involved and took much longer than setting up a type A machine. On average, we estimated that setup took about 20 percent more time. Also, consumables were much more expensive for type B, and maintenance took much longer. Precision and accuracy were much greater on the newer type B machines, but tight tolerances were not really an issue with our products and our customers. All in all, if the type A machines were given an efficiency rating of 100%, the type B managed barely 70%. Thus, the overall conclusion that we came to was that the versatility of the newer machines was overkill, because we did not have any customers who required products with these high tolerances. So in essence we had only one operation, but two distinctly different cost patterns, dependent on which route, that is A or B, was used to achieve what was fundamentally the same end result.

Obviously it would be a pity to lose the additional volume that had been generated by the doubling of capacity. So we investigated the cost implications of running two nine-hour shifts on a 24-hour basis on only the type A machines. All this still worked in our favor. The two type B machines were mothballed and put up for sale. There were only a few layoffs because most manufacturing personnel agreed to rotate from early to late shift in a two-week pattern. As you can imagine, the resultant "standardization" led to even more savings.

Suggestions from All Team Members

Personally, I have never been disappointed by asking employees at all levels to give me suggestions on how to be more efficient, cut costs, reduce wastage—or to tell me how they would improve the product. It's the premise mentioned in "Practice makes Perfect 4.1," namely, no one knows better how to do a task than the person who does it every day. One thing and one thing only is required: you must take all genuine suggestions very sincerely. That means that all of them are considered and discussed appropriately, with the proposer also, before they are adopted or rejected. If they are adopted, it's not a bad idea to give great publicity to this fact and provide some type of reward for the proposer. If the suggestion is rejected, it should be made quite clear as well why it was not thought suitable for implementation. It's not uncommon for older employees, particularly long-standing supervisors or managers, to feel threatened by suggestion boxes or open discussions on how to improve things. Either they feel guilty because they believe that they should have thought of those improvements themselves, or sometimes they even feel threatened because they feel the heat of young, eager competency and ambition on their necks. That's why it's important to create the right climate for such initiatives. I've often started by throwing up my hands and declaring, "It's all my fault; just blame me." Then convince everyone that the past is the past and cannot be changed, but what can be changed is what we do today. In a downturn that concept should not be too difficult to get across. The organizational climate should be right to solicit cooperation from all because survival is at stake. They more than likely know that anyway. Everyone can read between the lines; we all know that too, but back to the point: *everyone deserves to be asked to contribute to survival.*

Examine Staffing Costs Carefully

There are quite a few innovative schemes that can be adopted to reduce labor costs without actually shedding jobs. These include salary cuts, reduced hours, and forced vacations. An overall percentage cut in salaries across the board is perhaps the most directly visible one and, if feasible, has a well-defined savings rate. However, there are many more possibilities and opportunities in reduced working hours. First of all, during the long boom period, somewhat relaxed work practices, to put it mildly, have no doubt crept in. By reducing working hours without adjusting workload, you might very well find that, for example, with a payroll saving of 20%, productivity is reduced by much less, or sometimes even stays at the same level. The advantage is that nobody is singled out for redundancy, and in theory everyone suffers equally. After an initial adjustment phase, all personnel will get used to being more productive in less time, or, if you like, will be more productive and waste less time. Forced vacations are particularly efficient in production environments where stocks have built up to unacceptable levels due to a decrease in customer demand. Whether that approach is viable is dependent on the type of industry and the sometimes significant start-up costs associated with a lengthy shut-down period.

Somewhat more brutal, but pretty effective nevertheless, is this approach: during boom times, management might have found it a difficult internal sell to initiate a required shake-up and to reduce staff by, for example, 10%. Culling 10% of the lowest performers might even make the firm leaner by removing fat and yet not cutting into the muscle. However, depending on local labor laws, it might be quite a challenge for management to make 10% of the lowest performers redundant. Identifying them should be relatively easy, but "losing" them is a different matter altogether! This is particularly true in smaller companies, where the necessary preparatory work, such as performance appraisals, verbal and written warnings, and so forth, are not always in place.

Personnel Redundancies

If all the measures discussed above do not give you a significant improvement in your cash flow, you unfortunately will have to consider reducing your staff levels even more.[9] It's a fact of modern business life that personnel costs are the most significant operating costs in most organizations, and hence the greatest improvement to your cash flow can be achieved by a substantial reduction of your staff levels. If salary cuts, reduced working hours, and forced vacations will not provide the required balance between income and expenses, real redundancies must be faced.

This is an exercise that will tax your management team and you to the full because you will have to make decisions that will affect the lives of employees without consulting those employees. Also, you might have to make employees redundant who have done an excellent job for you, and that is not easy. So keep a tight lid on it until you have made a decision on who is going to stay, and who is going to go.

There is no easy way to tell a person that she has lost her job, particularly in a downturn; finding another one could prove pretty difficult. But in my experience the best way is to tell the person the bad news right away, hand her the written document, and then, only then, leave some time for discussion. Give the employee time to respond, and offer any help you are capable of giving. This can vary from elaborate outplacement solutions to helping with the compilation of résumés, providing references, and keeping your eye on opportunities for the unfortunate employees. But keep it short. There is no point in prolonging the agony, and the employee needs her own time to come to grips with the job loss.

The redundancy sessions should be held in as close a time span as possible. Bad news spreads like wildfire, and you want to get to the next step, addressing the survivors, as soon as possible. If feasible, hold all sessions yourself, but otherwise delegate them to as high a level as practicable. There needs to be absolutely no doubt as to the finality of the decision. If your organization has a personnel department, the relevant personnel manager can sit in, but the line manager has to do all the talking.

Unfortunately, Practice Makes Perfect 4.6
An Awful but Necessary Skill

Here is a suggested way to inform an employee, in this case Alan, that he is to be made redundant.

"Sit down please, Alan. I have some bad news for you; unfortunately your contract with us will be terminated as from today. This is no reflection on you or your performance, but a direct consequence of the difficult circumstances the company finds itself in. Naturally we will honor all our contractual obligations to you, but we would like you to collect your personal belongings from your locker (or desk) and leave the premises. We have put all this in a personal letter to you that I would like you to sign for receipt. There is a copy of this letter for your own records."

(Now give the employee some time to read the letter. If the employee asks whether there are other people made redundant say, "I'm afraid so.")

"Alan, this will no doubt come as quite a shock to you, so I want to say again that this decision was not made lightly and it is most certainly not a reflection on your work performance. I would also like to add that we will try to help you in any way possible to find another position. If you need a reference in the future, please feel free to contact me. Is there anything you would like to say at this stage?"

(Give the employee some time for a response, but don't go into long discussions. There is no turning back; you are informing him of an irreversible decision.)

"Thanks for those comments, Alan. Please feel free to contact me at any time if you feel that I can help you. Now, if you'll be so kind as to go with Mrs. X., she will accompany you. Make any phone calls you like from her office, but I would appreciate it if you could refrain from making any comments to your colleagues at this stage."

(Stand up and reach out for a handshake.)

"Alan, may I wish you the very best for the future, and don't forget my promise to you. Goodbye, Alan."

(Open the door for Alan, shake his hand again if appropriate, and then let Mrs. X. take over.)

This approach is pretty direct, and it probably needs to be modified in countries where a lot of seemingly irrelevant but socially important small talk is entered into before the main subject of the discussion is even reached. If there are cultural sensitivities, make sure you are aware of them, but do make the final message concise and clear!

Management Redundancies

Do not forget to look at your management structure and the possible savings to be realized from combining departments and rationalizing management positions. Professional staff departments are notoriously reluctant to give up their staff. But they are also the areas where contribution of an individual manager is difficult to determine, so force your departments to face reality. A long time ago when I ran a pretty large project in a remote location with a total staff of about 500 employees, the head office allocated me two cost engineers. After about a year, the project was postponed indefinitely by the client. All staff was laid off or transferred to other projects, and I was brought back to the head office. A month later, there were three cost engineers allocated to the postponed project. The VP of cost engineering did not want to lose any of his good people. He did not want to face the fact that drastic times call for drastic actions, and management structure has to be adapted to reflect a considerable decrease in activity. If sales drop by 70%, and there are no indications that this situation will recover in a hurry, you have to accept that your organization has been pummeled! You don't need a VP of Finance, or a VP for any other department for an organization that is a mere shadow of its former self. Survival means just that. It's very sad to lose good people, but it's even sadder to lose the company. I am not trying to be callous, but there are always more good people on the horizon. Don't ever forget that; there's no point in planning for the future if you haven't figured out yet how to pay next month's wages.

The Survivors

After the unfortunates have left, it is time to address the survivors. Tell them why it had to happen, and emphasize that you expect full cooperation in the difficult times to come. Don't promise that there won't be any more redundancy rounds. Let's be honest; conditions may get worse before they get better. Employees will have to learn to live with the uncertainty too. Human resources wisdom dictates that it's better to have one big redundancy round than a series of small ones. That is very nice to know, but not really very helpful in uncertain times. All you do know is what you know now, and the steps you have to take now to get the balance back between your cash in and cash out. In a couple of months you might be forced to take additional steps. One thing is for certain: in a downturn you have to take action with current facts and knowledge, not with what might or might not happen in the future. Do not assume that you can sit it out for one month, for two months, or for however many months. A downturn is just that, and chances are that the organization will have to keep on adapting to the ever-changing conditions.

MANAGE THE CASH FLOW AND YOUR BANK

In Chapter 1, we introduced the rediscovery of *cash* as a valuable commodity and introduced the term *burn rate*. The financial world, not unlike other disciplines, is full of jargon. However, there is a big difference between what I call concepts and facts. For example, *profit and loss* is a concept. It tries to indicate whether a company has achieved a positive or negative result over a period of time. There are a lot of assumptions and conventions hidden in this particular concept. It follows that all ratios derived from the *profit and loss* concept are concepts as well. For example, *earnings per share* (EPS) is a derived ratio from earnings, also known as profit, as is *earnings before interest and tax* (EBIT). All these accounting concepts and derived concepts can be useful for internal and external use to judge whether a company is doing well or not so well. That they have their limitations has been shown dramatically once more during the current (2009) downturn. Specifically, there are too many entries in accounting concepts that are wide open to interpretation, including *stock and asset values*. As managers, we have often pumped up the value of stock to make the balance sheet look a bit stronger, whereas recently the perceived and since-discovered unreal value of assets has had a devastating impact on the financial sector as a whole.[10] Contrary to accounting concepts, *real cash flow* (RCF) is a fact. The accounting interpretation of cash flow, namely, sources and application of funds, is again a concept derived from profit-and-loss and balance sheet entries, but RCF is fact. It's nothing more than the actual flow of money coming in, and the actual flow of money going out, that determines your RCF. And it's this factual movement, RCF, that determines whether you as a company will survive, struggle, or even perish in a downturn.

Real Cash Flow (RCF) is the Only Game in Town

It should come as no surprise to many of you that you can compare RCF with balancing your own checkbook. That's all there is to it, really, but as you also know by now, even on a personal level, the difficulty lies in the detail. In many companies the financial department is the generator and guardian of the cash flow. As cash flow is generated income-wise by sales, and expenditure-wise by purchases, wages, lease agreements, long-term commitments, and so forth, the point needs to be made that cash flow is everyone's business, never mind who keeps the score. In turn-around and difficult situations, I've often kept score myself, and discussed RCF continually with all relevant parties to signify how important it was. The lead-by-example principle has always been the main reason behind this DIY (do-it-yourself) activity. By making your RCF everyone's business, management has an easier task of explaining why guarding the cash flow is so critical to business survival. In most cases, the latter can be simplified by making all employees aware of the fact that getting paid for your services is everybody's business. Naturally, the reverse side of the coin, *savings,* is everybody's business as well!

Again, RCF has two and only two components: incoming and outgoing cash. Sounds easy enough, but unfortunately, in most cases, the incoming flow is difficult to predict, whereas the outgoing flow is difficult to stem. Let's look at outgoings first.

Stem the Cash Outflow

To get an accurate picture of cash going out in most companies is relatively straightforward. The only variables tend to be purchases for raw materials. Naturally these are tied, directly or indirectly, to sales. Most other expenditure is fairly constant at a given level of activity. That's why the so-called *burn rate,* the rate at which cash is consumed by paying creditors, including wages, can be determined relatively easily and accurately. It's more difficult to stem this constant flow of outgoing cash. One can start by examining stock levels, raw materials, secondary materials, office expenses, and so on, and work down those inventories to a more challenging level. Those items are already paid for, and they should generate some real savings, or generate income with regard to excess finished goods, in the short term.[11] Convert your scrap heap, yeah, the one at the bottom of the yard to cash, get rid of old machinery, and have a ball with old, unsalable stock; there is a customer for everything at the right price. This onetime cash injection to your cash flow will be very welcome indeed. Unnecessary or long-accepted overtime practices are other brakes that must be applied. They could reduce cost dramatically. Some examples of this were given under "Practice Makes Perfect 3.5."

More structured savings in outgoing cash often require major decisions, such as staff reductions, reducing lease payments by asset disposal, and so forth. Often these measures have no short-term benefit due to, for example, redundancy costs, penalties on terminating financial products, and so on. But in the longer term the decrease in activity level should lead to a lower burn rate. Be very thoughtful with supplier payments. Remind yourself of the dictum: *no suppliers = no products = no customers*. Find out what your suppliers' real terms of payments are, and try to stick with those. You don't want to get a reputation as a poor payer. After all, that will weaken your negotiation position considerably. If at the moment you really can't pay, communicate this fact to your supplier and make a plan. Your honest approach will most certainly appeal more that just giving him the brush-off time and time again.

Predict the Flow of Cash In

Predicting incoming cash is a real challenge for most companies. After all, incoming cash is directly related to estimated sales levels that are uncertain at the best of times and probably unreliable in difficult times. Nevertheless, every effort needs to be made to forecast cash in. This requires a fair amount of detail that needs to be looked at continually by everyone related to sales, or sales-related activities, such as service and installation, in your company. It can be helpful also to divide sales into regular, irregular, and incidental. Any separation that will focus on the detail and points to difficulties in a product range, particular type, and so on, will be helpful. Unless yours is a cash business, the next step is to make sure that invoices are produced promptly and correctly, and that customers pay within their credit terms. If they do, so much the better; if they don't, action is required.

Customers who don't pay on time fall into two categories, namely, those who *can't* pay and those who *won't* pay. Remember, times are tough, and you are not the only company trying to manage its cash flow. Customers who can't pay deserve special attention. Stay close to them and try to find out when they can pay. If you are in a supplier role, you have some leverage; After all, *no suppliers = no products = no customers* applies just as well to your customer. So make a plan, keep talking to the customer, and discuss possible staged payments. Be sure that you are at the top of the customer's payment list. That's where sound customer service, as discussed in the section "Concentrate on the

Practice Makes Perfect 4.7
Getting Paid—Everybody's Business

One thing that certainly becomes a lot more difficult in a downturn is getting paid on time by customers, sometimes even by very satisfied ones. That's why it's a good idea to reinforce with your own staff that getting paid is everybody's business. Put a procedure in place. For example,

1. Credit control alerts that an account is overdue. Credit control contacts sales and finds out whether everything went according to plan.
2. Sales checks with dispatch and transport and makes sure that all went well. If not, action is to be taken first to put things right. Credit control is put on hold.
3. If all is well, credit control contacts the accounts department of the customer and alerts that department to the overdue payment, asking when payment is to be made.
4. If after a specified period the account is still overdue, sales is alerted. The appropriate sales person speaks to her contact at the customer's company and tries to get commitment from this contact to pressure their accounts department to expedite payment.
5. If the account remains overdue, the financial manager speaks with his counterpart at the customer's company and tries to find out what is going on. He stresses that, according to his knowledge, there were no difficulties with products and deliveries. He tries to get a commitment for a payment by a certain date.
6. If payment is still not made, the general manager phones his counterpart at the customer's company and gets an audience. He stresses that payment should be made forthwith; otherwise he might have to consider putting further orders on hold. He stresses that there were no problems and that he would like to continue doing business with the customer's company. Also he tries to find out how the customer's company is faring.
7. If payment remains overdue without a commitment by the customer's company, all further orders are put on hold, and legal steps should be taken to try to recoup the debt.

All the steps listed should be executed in a very short time span. I've always used the following rule of thumb, assuming that credit terms are 30 days: steps 1, 2, and 3 within 5 days of being overdue; step 4 within 10 days; step 5 within 15 days; step 6 within 25 days; step 7 after

30 days of being overdue. It's critical to follow up consistently and to make it known that you are entitled to payment. Customers will soon realize that you take getting paid very seriously and they will probably put you high up on their "must get paid" list, particularly if you are one of their essential suppliers and have performed satisfactorily to date.

Big C," will really come into its own again. After all, your customer doesn't want to spoil a good relationship, and neither do you!

Customers who won't pay are normally associated with a real or perceived customer complaint. If possible, solve the problem, even if it takes some additional service or installation time, and remove the often-valid reason for nonpayment. Most customers will argue that you will try harder to address a complaint when they still hold on to a payment. And let's face it, most of the time they are right. If the customer is totally unhappy with the product, and you feel there is nothing more you can do, take the product back, and forget about it. It's also good customer service to acknowledge that some customers are beyond what your organization can offer. Leave them no argument to bad-mouth your company, and move on. Hopefully you have also learned to define a bit better who your real customers should be.

Manage the RCF

Trying to stem the outflow and predicting the inflow will be a fine balancing act in a downturn. That's where a simple cash flow statement that is kept up to date on a daily, weekly, or monthly basis, depending on the type of business, will help you decide who to pay and when on the basis of what has actually come in or is expected in shortly.[12] If you see troubles ahead, it's a good policy to phone an important supplier and tell him a few days before his payment is due that you are having some difficulties and would like an extension. Taking the initiative will put the supplier in the right frame of mind to grant such a request. If the supplier doesn't budge at all, it may be the right time to seek out other suppliers that market equivalent or compatible products.

When you get to the point where you can't possibly pay well-overdue supplier bills with the current cash flow, it is time for more drastic measures. One way is to write a formal letter to all your suppliers and explain what you propose to do; this needs to come across as a genuine plan to get out of difficulties. Also in this letter you need to tell them what internal measures you have taken or are about to take in order to get your own house in order. After all, the balance of incomings and outgoings needs to be restored as soon as possible. An example of such a letter is given below in "Practice Makes Perfect 4.8."

Practice Makes Perfect 4.8
When the Chips Are Really Down

To get over an exceptionally serious cash flow crisis, it sometimes pays to ask your suppliers for cooperation. The following letter is an example of how you could approach all your suppliers.

Dear Madam or Sir,

It has probably not gone unnoticed that we are currently having some difficulties paying your outstanding invoices. Unfortunately, this situation is not going to improve in the short term. We are currently experiencing some serious difficulties, and we would very much like your help in getting on top of these problems. Therefore, we would ask you to agree to the following:

- All overdue invoices will not require payment for the moment. In your case, this concerns invoices . . . for a total amount of $. . . .
- All current invoices, 30 days or less, will be paid when due out of our current cash flow.
- All agreements with regard to discounts, delivery terms, and so forth, will remain in force. In particular I refer to . . .
- Our current pricing, including volume discounts, will remain as is. Reference is made to . . .
- All overdue invoices will be paid at a rate of 10% each month until they are fully paid.

We are also taking extensive internal measures to overcome our difficulties, including substantial salary cuts for me and my management team. Therefore, I would ask you to sign this proposal for acceptance and return it to me. If there is any further information you require, please don't hesitate to contact me. We are confident that with your help and our internal measures we can return to a normalized situation within . . . months. Trusting that this proposal can meet with your agreement and looking forward to your positive reaction, Seen and Accepted

Yours Truly, (Signed by Customer)   (Signed by General Manager)

Why does this have a chance of success? Like yourself, your suppliers don't want to see you going out of business. After all, they will lose a customer. As long as there is a reasonable chance of your survival, they would like you to succeed. Naturally this type of approach is a last stand, and conditions need to be agreed to by your suppliers and honored by you. If you don't see a way out at all, say so and wind up the business if it's yours to wind up. Again, honesty will be remembered, and who knows what will happen in the future when you try again.

Manage Your Bank

Last but not least is the management of your bank. This assumes that you have a working capital facility that is an integral part of your cash flow. If not, so much the better; forget this section and move on! Unfortunately most companies will have to rely on some form of working capital funding, such as invoice discounting or overdraft facilities from their bankers. During normal times, your bank account manager will more than likely demand a certain amount of information to satisfy herself and her powers that be that your business is solvent. In difficult times you can take the initiative by supplying more information. In particular, the latest (2008–?) downturn has made banks very cautious and well aware of the fact that they themselves are under observation as to their own viability. This is not the time to be creative with your bank; it's the time to give them as much confidence as possible that you are holding your own in a downturn. So communicate with them, give them information about your customer base, explain how ordering patterns are holding up and your continued success with some of your suppliers; detail your efforts to improve quality, your newest service initiatives, your pains to reduce costs, or your inverse marketing program. In the past I have done all this with a formal letter that accompanied a required monthly cash flow statement. It doesn't take that much time, it shows initiative rather than waiting for the bank to ask, and it makes for excellent public relations. As most companies won't do this (we're all a bit weary of bankers, you know), you will be the beautiful exception that imprints on your banker's mind. Remember, it's all in the detail and in the mind.

A last point that is worth considering concerns your existing credit lines. If you have existing credit lines, or a revolving credit arrangement that was set up some time ago at a favorable rate, but that is not yet used to the full, it might be an idea to draw it down completely, even if you don't need it right now. New credit might be pretty difficult to get hold of in the near future.

MANAGE YOUR PUBLIC PROFILE

The quantity of information available from public companies undoubtedly gives real meaning to the word *public*. Batteries of analysts, journalists, and other interested parties monitor, predict, and report on the ups and downs of public companies. CEOs of public companies spend a great amount of their time on public relations and other external activities to promote their organizations. It's almost a full-time job, particularly in recent times when some of these captains of industry have reached celebrity status. Large private companies do not attract the same amount of attention, whereas small private companies tend not to even think about their public profiles. However, there is information in the public domain or the private sphere that can have a significant influence on your operations, namely, your credit rating.

Optimize Your Credit Rating

Private companies in the United States are not obliged to register publicly, as opposed to their counterparts in Europe. The latter must register at their regional chamber of commerce and supply annual accounts for the public domain. In the United States, similar but wholly privatized databases exist through companies such as Dun & Bradstreet, Equifax, and so forth. These credit-rating agencies track companies' credit worthiness, determine credit scores or credit ratings, and sometimes even handle collections. They get their information on a voluntary basis, whereas some businesses pay for featured listings or advanced services. Also, they will set up profiles for any company that they come across in the course of their collection services.[13] The chances are that in the United States, for medium-sized private companies anyway, and in Europe for all private companies, a credit rating has been determined and is available by means of a paid service or public records, respectively. It's this credit rating that is used by your suppliers to grant your company a certain line of credit. Your credit rating is also the reason why sometimes your company has no chance of doing business with a new client, because unknown to you, the credit rating makes that potential client nervous. No one will ever tell you, but that's why credit is a hidden but oh-so-real obstacle in contract negotiations. Particularly in a downturn, the services of credit-rating agencies are used in almost all significant transactions. Nobody wants to do business with a potential credit risk! Obviously you cannot really manipulate your audited accounts or other information available to private credit-rating agencies, but there are some ways in which you can at least have some influence on what is being published and when.[14]

The Credit Rating Itself

For public and large companies, a credit rating is based on all the public and perhaps not-so-public information that the credit-rating agency feels is important. Credit-rating agencies have certainly been in the news of late with regard to overoptimistic ratings for certain companies and complex financial products. For smaller companies there tends to be only one overriding ingredient that determines your credit rating, and that is shareholders' funds. By itself, that is not surprising, given the limited information that is available in general for smaller companies. Most credit-rating agencies will allocate your company a credit rating of about 10% of shareholders' funds.[15] That is what they consider relatively safe, and that is what you have to live with. Knowing this, it stands to reason that, if you can pump up your company's shareholders' funds, you will improve its credit rating. A simple example might illustrate the possibilities. As a shareholder/director you could inject $100,000 into your company by means of a personal loan, or alternatively as capital. A loan will have no effect on your company's credit rating, but a capital injection will pump up this rating by $10,000! So what's the difference? The straightforward answer is tax. A loan can be paid back to a director without incurring income tax for her. Unfortunately, if you want to withdraw the injected capital, you are subjected to income tax. Hence, just about all accountants will recommend the tax-efficient route; after all, they are not in the credit-rating business. But here is the point—surely you should be able to decide for yourselves what route is the most beneficial? If you are in business for the long haul, a much improved credit rating might just give your organization that slight edge in the unspoken stakes of creditworthiness during contract negotiations! Injecting capital also gives a clear signal to the marketplace that you, the directors/shareholders, are committed.

Other information that forms part of a company's file, publicly or privately held, and that could influence its credit rating, includes court injunctions against it. In most countries, once such legal actions have been registered, they are not automatically removed. So they will be part of your public profile until you instigate the removal! Therefore, if the company has cleared the charge against it, make sure that you get the injunction removed by paying a small fee and informing the court and the credit-rating agency.

Publicity Opportunities

The last point that needs to be discussed under your public profile is the opportunities that do arise to put your company in the limelight. Whether it is the local, national, or international press, treat them all with kid gloves. Politicians don't say for nothing, "Treat every microphone like it's live." The same can be said for journalist interviews. If possible, tell the journalist that you want final say on what is to be printed or broadcasted. Untold damage can be done by a loose remark, a flippant statement, or a thoughtless comment. Don't give live interviews unless you are well used to it! Even the "sending you the questions that will be discussed" ploy will not stop a journalist who smells sensation! The modern power of the media can condemn your business with a glib headline or a five-minute, hard-hitting radio interview before you can blink an eyelid. In the past I've always tried to answer the following questions for myself: why do they want to talk, and what has happened lately that suddenly gives them an interest in little old me.

That's not to say that you should not use opportunities to promote your company. Just be wary at all times of the possible twist to the tail. It's much easier to be well prepared and get it straight the first time than to bend over backward to correct what you shouldn't have said in the first place.

BATTEN DOWN THE HATCHES, BUT STAY THE COURSE

To reinforce all the measures that you have taken to protect your cash flow also requires incorporation of the adjustments to your existing policies and procedures. It sounds like a small point, and perhaps it is, but it tends to reinforce the new reality. Again you must assume that the downturn is going to last a while, and it is always easier to relax a rule at a later stage. Policies that come to mind are purchasing policies and human resources policies. They are the ones most concerned with expenditure, so if you have taken steps in these areas, you should communicate them formally to all staff. Then, you guessed it, follow up and make sure the new policies are adhered to. It's in the detail, the routine daily detail, again and again.

Purchasing Policies

In difficult times one needs to turn over every penny before it is committed. Yes, I use the word committed because there are far too many organizations that control purchase payments after a commitment has been entered into. You can't really control the cash flow by delaying payment of services and goods received. You can manipulate it by postponing it, but you cannot control it. Control means that you introduce the question, do we need it, and how much do we need it, before you make the actual commitment at the appropriate time. It's also not a bad idea to move all purchasing decisions one level up the organization for additional scrutiny. Make it well known that your purchasing procedure has changed. Even your suppliers might have to be informed. I've been confronted with situations where employees just went to a particular supplier and purchased whatever they thought they needed with the magic words, "just put it on ABC's account." An extreme example perhaps, but nevertheless taken from recent practice. Also the raw materials supplier that just made five deliveries a day needs to be whistled back. You can't expect him to be concerned about your business; that is your own business! So inform him, introduce strict control, and check that you get what you ordered, both with respect to quality and quantity. Don't allow any exceptions. If you allow some exceptions, relaxed practices will soon infiltrate again. Remember, it's all in the detail and the follow-up!

Human Resources Policies

Having reduced your staff levels is not the end, I'll promise you. The demands of supervisors and department heads will soon resurface because any excuse will be found to try to reintroduce the previous comfortable status quo. The premise for this is quite straightforward: it's easy to give something to people; it's much more difficult to take something away, and then let the person get used to managing without. So if there were six accounts clerks, and, after rationalization, there are four, you will hear plenty of stories of not coping, work stress, slave driving, and so forth. Don't react too quickly. A new equilibrium has to be found. In good times it wasn't only your bottom line that kept improving. Workers were also getting used to a more relaxed working environment. After all, things were going pretty well. So the reality shock needs a bit of time to dissipate before everyone gets used to new realities.

Because of its cost implications, it's probably very appropriate to put a stop to recruitment. That means that any request, even a replacement request, needs to go right to the top for consideration. Make that very clear. I've learned through bitter experience that replacement recruitment was "surely not included in the recruitment stop; After all, we are only replacing Mrs. X, who has left." At this difficult stage of play, sometimes an internal or lateral move can be made rather than introduce a new employee. You are also giving a very useful and valid signal, namely, our own people come first. Maybe it's not the "95 percent" solution that the supervisor or manager wants, but the "75 percent plus on-the-job training" one. Advertise internally and evaluate. Although most organizations have human resources databases, they are seldom set up or used effectively to identify potential and latent skills. In my own experience I have come across factory workers with bookkeeping diplomas, secretaries with pretty useful practical sales experience, a shuttering carpenter with a law degree, and even an office cleaner with a master's degree in anthropology. Don't assume anything; just get information and evaluate. Know your people, talk to them, and be pleasantly surprised. There is a lot more stretch and know-how in an organization than most managers know about or want to admit to, and now is the time to find it out.

Product and Service Quality

If there is one thing that should never be compromised on or tampered with, it is quality. Nowadays product quality tends to be a given and is no longer a marketable parameter. For that very reason, there is much emphasis on brands in advertising, but quality is seldom mentioned anymore. Customers expect quality from any product, whether it is a well-known brand, a price-competitive equivalent, or a relatively cheap, comparable product. Manufacturing and assembly techniques tend to be similar anyway. Often the test of time is totally superfluous and has been replaced by the endless introduction of new "improved" models, next season's fashions, or the "throw-away" concept.

Service quality is a much more difficult concept. It depends very much on what is being serviced and how visible the particular service is. However, the basic premise should always be that you do not tamper with your accepted and established service levels. If at all possible you should ratchet up your service levels during a downturn to reinforce that your service is part of the total sales package, and customers can rely on it at all times. Don't even think of taking shortcuts in quality in order to save on manufacturing costs and expenses.

Stay the Course

It's crucial during hard times to make sure that you do not deviate from your company objectives unless there are very, very compelling reasons. Then and only then make a deliberate course change, and stick to it once more. Zigzagging and circling get you nowhere in a hurry, and you can safely assume that nobody is waiting around to torpedo your business because it is following a straight course. Nothing is more disconcerting to employees than to be confronted by continually changing directives from the top. You can't change a make or buy decision every fourteen days because of currency fluctuations. You can't tell plant A that they will lose Product XX to Plant B, and change your mind again a week later. You can't say that you are stopping all overtime and then ask half of the employees to work overtime just this once, on more than one occasion. You can't change your discount policy every second day and then blow up because one of your staff sold at the wrong discount, and so on. This type of panic reaction will get you nowhere. Staff will eventually become lax in carrying out your latest brain wave, or your latest "must be obeyed or else . . ." directive, and you will lose credibility and commitment. Nothing is worse than to realize that no one takes your pronouncements seriously any more. Particularly in difficult times, you need to act as if you are fully in control, know what you are doing, and encourage everyone else to stay the course with you. Don't spend too much time on strategy or in your office behind your computer; you can do that at night or at home. Just concentrate on getting things done and being consistent. Now is the time to lead from the front, be seen, encourage, correct, compliment, and do all the things that make employees feel that they are all part of the same team. In the end, it is the team that must stay the course and succeed as a team.

Customer Relations Once More

Obviously it is fitting to end this chapter on a note similar to its beginning. It all starts with the customer, the big C, and it ends with her too. The black box in between, all the things that a business has to do to satisfy her, is not in the least bit interesting for her. As long as she gets what was ordered on time, in good condition, and presented with a smile, we will have the best chance of her coming back. That will allow us to get all worked up again to what happens in the black box we call our organization. All the intricate systems that are so necessary to produce the end product are our concern and our concern alone. After all, we are not particularly interested in the black boxes of our suppliers, as long as they deliver what we ordered in good condition and on time. That's why we refer to these intricacies as the black box. So whatever we do, we do it all for the big C. Let there never be any doubt about that.

The Basics Summarized

1. It's all in the detail.
2. Perfect, practical, and honest customer service.
3. Selling is key.
4. Lead by example.
5. Ask yourself the question, how can we add value?
6. Concentrate on RCF (the Real Cash Flow).
7. Your organization has nothing to lose but a client.
8. Every employee deserves to be asked to contribute to survival.
9. Start to reappraise how value is added, which parts of your business are viable, and which are not.
10. Your customers don't care what goes on in your black box.
11. Stay the course and be consistent.

CHAPTER 5

THERE MUST BE OPPORTUNITIES OUT THERE

I find the harder I work, the more luck I seem to have.
—Thomas Jefferson (1743–1826)

LOOK AROUND AND KNOW WHAT IS GOING ON

During a downward trend, there is so much bad news that we often forget to consider our own environment first. The "noise" of the macroeconomic signals, as transmitted by the media, tries to condition us that things are bad, and we must be prepared for even worse. Next moment we observe that the media have changed their headlines from "coping with the downturn" to "the road to recovery," but we haven't noticed any material change in our own business environment. What is going on, and how useful is all of this? One of the characteristics of the modern media is that they know they have to change their tune frequently to retain the short attention span of viewers and listeners. Most of the data that is being dished up is totally irrelevant to our daily business life. We can't influence this or do anything about it; it's nothing but noise that might put us in a certain frame of mind, but that's about all.

It's a fast-paced world out there, or is it? In our own business environment we can't afford to have the short attention span or superficial interest that the media seem to assume and propagate. Whether this is a pull or push marketing phenomenon is a moot point. After all, if a lot of us would no longer watch or read what is being dished up, the media would soon change their own business model. However, for our own business use we need relevant information, as opposed to endless data. We need useful information that affects our business and that requires some type of action now or in the future. What we need to do is filter information more effectively into local information, expected trends, and government interference.

Local Information

As a retailer in a shopping mall, you notice that just about everyone displays big signs in their windows: 60% off; buy one, get two free, and so forth. That's local information. What do you do? You operate a large service station on a very busy road. In one of the local newspapers you note that work on the long-planned bypass is starting next week, as part of the government's plan to stimulate infrastructure works. What do you do? Or, you run a very successful local engineering company, and you have just heard that a major competitor will open a branch not far from you. What do you do? All the above are just random examples of how important local news can be for small- to medium-sized enterprises, and lest we forget, those still comprise close to 50% of GDP in the United States and the UK—and still more in other countries.[1]

But even for multinationals, local news is important. *Local* in their context probably means country or region. After all, the term *local* is relative to

---

Practice Makes Perfect 5.1
Reconnoiter Before You Act

A recent report in a Dutch newspaper, *De Telegraaf,* 11 April 2009, about a German ex-soldier who felt guilty after 64 years (better late than never) and wanted to make amends for stealing a bicycle outside a church in a little Dutch village in the dying days of the war, reminded me of the following personal story.[2]

My dad, who died peacefully at the ripe old age of 90+, some years ago, never told us kids anything much of the war years, apart from this tale.

During the last three years of the German occupation, he had kept a bicycle, taken apart, hidden in a secret place in the attic. The Germans were constantly looking for "free" civilian assets to supplement their own. In the first days of May 1945, the Germans were in full retreat with the end of the war close at hand, but not yet formally announced. My dad couldn't wait, assembled his bicycle, and went for a ride. What luxury after three years of walking! The German troops had supposedly left a few days earlier, according to the national news bulletins, anyway. Not far from home, much to his surprise, Dad came across a forlorn German soldier who pointed his rifle at my dad and commandeered his bicycle. My dad objected and said, "But the war is over!" To which the German replied, "But not for you, mate." Then he mounted the bicycle and rode off.

---

your own business environment. For example, in Belgium, the vast majority of cars sold have diesel engines. How many diesel engine cars are sold in the United States and Canada? Why do you think some products change their names, packaging size, method of packaging, and so forth, across borders? It's not only marketing, but also local knowledge that dictates that a certain name or packaging size is inappropriate.

Local knowledge is readily available, but you need to make sure that you have all your senses well tuned to pick it up and use it to your company's benefit. That listening to customers is tops in gaining local information should no longer come as a surprise.

Expected Industry Trends

It's a lot more difficult to know what to do with expected trends. In the short term, probably nothing, but in the medium-to-longer term it might be useful to test some of those trends if you are in a position to, or alternatively watch very closely and be prepared to "follow" rapidly. For example, it's an unproven fact that markets tend to shake out mature products and favor untested and exciting new ones in a downturn. There's probably just as much "proof" that customers favor established reliable products over unproven ones in difficult times. The problem with most of this type of "research" is that correlations and standard deviations of the results of the sample groups would make a mathematician splutter, stutter, and probably mutter hysterically, if that is possible.[3] Unfortunately we are kept ignorant of these important indicators; instead we are fed another headline. For example, "'new' U.S. shopper [value for money] to emerge from crisis" and "economic climate shifts consumers online."[4] The first report was based on a sample of 500 people in the United States, the UK, and France, and a number of other "no samples mentioned" surveys, and the second one on just over 4000 online shoppers on a comparison Web site. So, do we now rush out, upgrade and redesign our Web sites, and get rid of all our luxury products? I trust not! It's a bit of uncontrolled research, that's all. Consumer behavior research is pretty unreliable at the best of times, so I hate to know what its likely accuracy is in bad times. Does that mean we need to dismiss it out of hand? I would think not!

Conventional wisdom suggests that consumers return to their old spending habits once a recession abates. Pent-up demand will unleash a gigantic buying spree! Will this happen as a matter of course? No two downturns are the same, so be very careful with this type of "historically based prediction." It is not unlike the sales forecast and budget parallel: great in quiet, predictable times, but absolutely useless during major upheavals. A much-quoted saying during my business school years in the 1980s was "Chartists are Charlies," and it is as well to keep that at the back of your mind.[5]

That's where our own business common sense should dictate the short-term approach and our own reaction. To me it's pretty logical that consumers in general will be more careful in difficult times. Will that be a lasting trend? It's anybody's guess, but it's worth keeping it in the back of your mind. Will people start using the Web for comparative price shopping? More and more, no doubt. Which Web sites will be the winners? Difficult to predict; there is hardly need for 10 national Web sites comparing home and car insurances for eligible consumers.

The very best statistics and trends are your own sales numbers and your own consumer research, such as repeat business, new customers, and customer complaint frequencies. If you listen and stay close to your customers, you might even pick up a real trend that is important to your business and to your location.

Government Interference

One of the worst consequences of a serious downturn is government inter-ference. The rule here appears to be if you fail, fail big, and government will come to your aid. The current downturn (2008–?) is a stark reminder. We keep on hearing that the banking sector is not allowed to fail. It's too important for the economy. What about all those banks that did not get involved in those trendy new products. Should they not be rewarded by an influx of new cus-tomers because they held to their core business? And if the financial sector was so important to the economy as a whole, why did our governments not control it much more tightly and strictly? In the ordinary business world the punish-ment for bad performance is insolvency or being fired. What is the punishment for malpractice and insolvency in financial circles? Why was money pumped into a bloated worldwide car industry, with an estimated overcapacity of 74%? Would the money not have been much better spent on retraining workers, improving public transport, developing communication networks, and sup-porting small businesses? The latter, by the way, are still the largest contributors to employment. These are all questions begging for answers that might never be provided. No great help to your business, either, if it finds itself adversely influenced by government aid dished out to very large competitors.

So what can you do? Precious little, I'm afraid. In the early 2000s in a European country, a very large building contractor hit the wall. Government interfered big-time, with the net result that the very large contractor got work with silly, tender prices and survived with government aid packages, and a crowd of medium construction companies went bust. The irony was that a couple of years later what should have happened much earlier happened anyway. In our Western economies, inefficiencies will eventually be eliminated; with government aid it just takes longer and tends to waste considerable amounts of taxpayers' money. Anything to secure votes—remember the reelection objective of politicians?

So if you are in an industry where the really big boys get government support, try to get a slice of the pie as well. Just beware that your emphasis does not shift from the customer to focusing on getting hold of government aid. Particularly for small and medium businesses, any distraction from a strong customer focus might prove to be much more lethal than concentrating on what looks like a free lunch. Just remind yourself of the saying, "there is no such thing as a free lunch."

The opportunity in all of this lies in the early recognition of new consumer sentiment or a new trend and then deciding how your business can benefit. *Thus, opportunity number one has to be, filter out the noise, but be very well informed so you can use developing trends or sentiments to your benefit.*

INVERSE MARKETING IS FUN

Let's first of all explain the rationale behind *Inverse marketing*. Inverse marketing is a term that I use to describe good purchasing practices.[6] Perhaps it smacks a bit of title inflation, but it's done with a purpose as well. Namely, it's very effective to be reminded that what you are trying to do for your customers, including marketing, customer services, and all the other things that were described in the previous chapters, your suppliers are vigorously trying to do for you—probably with the same effectiveness as you are applying to your own customers. Does it not stand to reason that you can behave as a customer in this scenario? That last part is so obvious, therefore it is often forgotten and certainly not used to advantage. Management is so geared toward customers and marketing that purchasing is delegated without too much attention and interference. Of course, customers are the overriding consideration, but you can't abdicate the back end so blatantly!

In quite a few organizations that I have worked with, purchasing was considered to be a necessary evil by the powers that be. Sometimes the top didn't even get involved in purchasing decisions, certainly not in the ones for secondary materials, such as packaging, spare parts, office supplies, and so forth. I have even been with organizations where primary materials were purchased by the purchasing department without any real controls. The owner-manager told me that he kept an eye on the quoted prices for raw materials in the newspaper. As long as the factory got its supplies, he was happy. And that leads us to the real secret of inverse marketing. You can't delegate it to your purchasing department. You will have to get involved from time to time; that is the real secret. The regular contact between your purchasing department and the supplier sales force has to be shaken in order to get some real results. The cozy, comfortable, regular contact between your purchasing manager and the supplier sales force needs to be temporarily interrupted, queried, and then reestablished for regular business. Inverse marketing is not a regular daily activity, a bit of discount here and a bit of discount there, but an exercise to find out whether you are still getting value for money from your suppliers and to cement a relationship for a certain period of time. After the exercise is completed, and controls are put in place to monitor agreements, the inverse marketing job is done until next time.

Real, Undiluted Savings

Let's now examine the real benefit of an inverse marketing campaign. It's so obvious that it needs to be spelled out in order to let it sink in properly, namely, savings on your raw materials and supplies drop straight down to your bottom line. No additional effort, no additional cost, just undiluted savings. What you see is what you get, no questions about it. To generate an additional dollar of sales, most companies have to expend considerable energy, such as marketing and sales, manufacturing and distribution, and so on. If your usual net profit is 25%, then you can assume with some degree of confidence that you will keep 25 cents for every extra dollar in sales generated.

But a dollar saved at the front end, on your raw materials and supplies, translates directly to your bottom line. No extra effort, no dilution, this dollar slips through your black box and remains a dollar. You might not see it, but your RCF, real cash flow, will feel it and benefit accordingly. If that is not an opportunity to be exploited, I don't know what is. What is even more exciting is that you are in control, you are the customer, and you are "the opportunity" for your existing supplier and his competitors. You can have your cake and eat it, then savor the cherry on top by recognizing that *every dollar saved goes straight to the bottom line.*

Supplier Power Reduced

It's not uncommon for suppliers to be much larger than their customers. Particularly in manufacturing and construction, suppliers of the raw materials are often hiding behind *quoted market or industry pricing,* a nice name for a cartel. This supplier power can be challenged successfully, and probably even more so in a downturn. The more prestigious, or, if you like, intimidating, the supplier's reputation, the more vulnerable the supplier is to a determined

Practice Makes Perfect 5.2
Inverse Marketing in Practice

An inverse marketing campaign starts off by getting the cooperation of your purchasing department. Assure them that whatever comes out is no reflection on their past performance or their capabilities. But this campaign is initiated by you, the general manager, for maximum effect. They will naturally be involved in the evaluations and final decision. (In my experiences, if there are violent objections from a purchasing manager, the chances are that the campaign will have great benefits!)

Step 1. An official letter is composed and sent from you to all the general managers of suppliers capable of fulfilling your requirements for particular materials or products. Politely state that you are currently reviewing all supplier agreements with a view to optimizing your inputs to your own operations. It must be a detailed letter with specifications, tolerances, delivery frequency, expected quantities, and so forth. You ask the potential suppliers to quote as comprehensively as possible, with pricing, volume discounts, transport costs, and so forth, and to respond by a certain date. Don't give them too much time!

You will now find that the phones in the purchasing department will start ringing! The existing supplier salesmen want to know what is going on. Are we not happy? What has gone wrong? Or any number of similar questions. Sometimes they will even offer a substantial discount right away. Your brief to the purchasing department is quite clear: unfortunately, there is nothing they can do. This is an exercise initiated by the CEO or general manager, but if they want to offer discounts, please incorporate it in their response, and so forth. Potential suppliers will try to contact you looking for a face-to-face meeting, but they are all asked politely to reply in writing. All additional detail that is requested is to be supplied in writing as well.

Step 2. When all the quotes have been received by the due date, the evaluations can begin. All companies that supplied quotes are thanked in writing and informed that the company is looking to wrap it all up by a certain date. After the evaluations are complete, a second round is undertaken. This round is primarily meant for the existing supplier. (Practice teaches that most new suppliers, if they are keen to get the business, will have given a pretty competitive effort. The present supplier is normally the one that needs to be convinced that you are serious and prepared to change.) In a second official letter you inform all respected parties that very competitive quotes have been received, and therefore everyone is asked to review his original quote once more. Again a time limit is set.

Step 3. A final evaluation is undertaken, and a decision is made. The chosen supplier, not necessarily the cheapest one, is asked to attend a meeting to iron out any additional difficulties and to negotiate a final deal. Don't ever forget rule number one of negotiating skills: *"The worst you can do with any negotiator is to accept his first offer."* It stands to reason that negotiators want to negotiate. If a first offer is acceptable, what other offer might have been acceptable if it had been tried? So in actual fact the acceptance of a first offer tends to undermine confidence in the deal and in oneself.

If for whatever reason you are not happy, you can invite the second choice supplier and repeat step 3. Then and only then is a final decision made. Agreements are signed, and the agreement is bedded down with the purchasing department. This last part is pretty important because sometimes formally negotiated supplier agreements can be quite detailed if there are quite a few products and varieties involved. For example, different packaging and sizes, different prints, different materials, different quantities, and so on. Make sure that the agreement is well understood, and then follow up. It's again in the detail.

---

inverse marketing campaign. Suddenly you will find that *if you behave like a customer and not like a producer who needs his materials, that is, if you practice inverse marketing (it's all in the mind, you know),* that there is always more than one supplier and, believe it or not, other suppliers are keen to have you as a customer. So don't be worried about the reaction of your current supplier to your inverse marketing push. Your supplier's salesmen will be all over your purchase department to find out whether there's something wrong, and what they can do—even offer immediate discounts, and so forth. Brief your purchase department, and have them tell suppliers that senior management is doing a review of purchasing practices and it's out of their hands. I've come across indignation, even arrogance, but never, repeat, never, has a supplier withdrawn from what is to follow, namely a chance to keep or get your business. If you are worried that your existing supplier will "get even," realize that your supplier is even more worried than you are. Remember, you are a customer, and nobody likes to lose one! So if ever there was a time to test the market and get your materials at the best possible price with your specifications and delivery requirements, this is it! Now don't for one minute think that inverse marketing suggests that you change supplier. All inverse marketing wants to achieve is getting value for your money. What actually constitutes value, you can decide for yourself like all good customers. *Decide* is the operative word here.

Just Try It and Be Surprised

In just about all organizations that I have been associated with I've introduced and practiced inverse marketing. Every time, the results were amazing. By breaking open existing, often long-term, supplier relations, a great deal of money was saved. But here is the real clincher—in most instances the existing suppliers reduced charges. But not always. My classic case to demonstrate one of these exceptions goes as follows. It dates back awhile, but it revolved around a manufacturer that was situated in the same industrial area as its main supplier for its main raw material. Deliveries to us were very erratic, and they had to be followed up continuously. We were not one of their main customers, and it showed! When I got around to the inevitable inverse marketing campaign, the owners said to me, no hope: all the other suppliers can't compete with transport costs; we just have to live with it. Nevertheless, we went through the motions of round one and, surprisingly enough, there was a supplier that came in with a 9% reduction in price, including transport, for a minimum contract of a year. The existing supplier did not even bother to respond, but informed the purchasing manager that existing pricing could not be adjusted. When we asked that supplier in round two to please review its price in view of competing bids, the company ignored us totally. When their representatives saw deliveries being made by their competitor, they woke up! Nothing in business is chiseled in stone, and everything should be negotiable.

In difficult times, the practice of inverse marketing should certainly be part of your repertoire of looking for opportunities. Don't forget that by saving substantial amounts on the front end, you might be more competitive on the back end. So without any reservation, *opportunity number 2 is to apply inverse marketing in support of marketing.*

Don't Buy Twice

One of the reasons why an inverse marketing campaign often results in doing business with your existing suppliers, but on better terms, is no doubt the inherent difficulties of change. Of course there are big differences here. For example, a stationery supplier is a distributor of goods. Even unbranded goods are "branded," nowadays, meaning that they come from the same producer. So changing a stationery supplier is probably not that great a deal. A supplier that machines a small part to very high tolerances for your subassembly, a part that in turn goes to an engine manufacturer, and eventually ends up in a light aircraft is a different kettle of fish. Don't let that deter you! It means more effort needs to be put into finding alternative suppliers that fulfill your requirements. When you do find such suppliers, you will have to subject them to a lengthy period of quality assurance testing. That should be daily fare in a lot of companies anyway, to find out which suppliers can fulfill your exact requirements.

If the inverse marketing campaign shows up really substantial savings, alarm bells should start ringing. That doesn't mean that one should not go for the much better deal, but that one should be extra careful and investigate further. That has nothing to do with the practice of inverse marketing, but everything to do with making absolutely sure that what you are going to get is what you actually require. We have all been caught by the real cheap gadget that fell to bits when you looked at it long and hard. But I, for one, have also been caught by the big name brand that looked oh-so-great, but that gave up the ghost soon afterward. There are no rules, only your company's requirements and its considered expert judgment of value for money.

Delicately Balanced Supply Chains?

It has been suggested to me recently (2009) that inverse marketing leads to bad purchasing practices because modern, sophisticated supply chains are very delicately balanced and need cooperation between client and supplier, rather than alienating them. In Chapter 2, under "The Streets are Not Paved with Gold—JIT Is on Hold," we mentioned the fact that suppliers might put larger companies in difficulties because they are cash strapped as well— witness the car industry. Surprise, surprise! According to some press reports, large carmakers are bending over backward to help suppliers keep delivering. In hindsight, relentlessly squeezing suppliers in sophisticated supply chains was not the answer. Now, before we all start feeling sorry for these goliaths of industries, let's get a few things straight.

Balanced for Whom?

First, inverse marketing is not a mechanism to relentlessly squeeze suppliers. It's a method to find out whether you are getting value for money from your current suppliers. The difference between value and price, as we discussed previously, is in the eye of the beholder. The concept of getting value for money gives you the obligation to examine pricing from your current suppliers for the benefit of your own bottom line, your employees, and your shareholders.

Second, the very large consumer companies—carmakers, retailers, and so forth, are much bigger than their suppliers. Generally speaking, this is not the case for most companies and industries, where most suppliers tend to be much larger than their customers.

Third, these large consumer companies have been squeezing their much smaller suppliers for quite some time, until there was precious little left to squeeze. Suppliers of these powerful conglomerates were confronted with open-book demands to make sure that they were holding nothing back and didn't make too much profit. I have been there and seen this on a number of occasions—for example, the arrogance of a supermarket chain that informed me that we had to "shave" another 0.5 cents off our product; otherwise we would lose half our existing shelf space. So now, in a downturn, there is nothing more to squeeze out of these "exist by the grace of your customer" suppliers that had precious little in the way of reserves in any case!

Fourth, JIT was a system invented and propagated by and for these large consumer companies. It did put the onus of keeping buffer stocks squarely in the orbit of the supplier. After all, not delivering was often punished financially. The idea that everyone can produce just enough to satisfy demand is assuming that demand is accurately known and forecast. This wonder world is feasible only when demand outstrips supply, when trends are predictable, and in the theoretical models of consultants. Hence, it is an efficient system designed for a boom period that gets pretty unreliable during a downturn.

Fifth, inverse marketing tries to establish a longer-term formal relationship with a supplier, thereby benefitting the supplier as well. Most companies have no formal relationships with their much larger suppliers, and they are often bullied to accept "market price or industry" increases. It's too easy for the supplier, and it should be challenged from time to time in an orderly and effective fashion.

Last, we are all being conditioned to accept what is on offer. The old art of negotiation has almost disappeared. That's certainly true in many European countries where "big brother" tries to regulate just about everything from setting professional fees to the price of a loaf of bread. On top of this, industry organizations publish elaborate booklets to precondition us as to what price is associated with new and used goods. The very latest ones are the mushrooming comparison Web sites that "make it easier" to compare all types of products and services. They offer comparisons galore, all made available to condition us into accepting the so-called *realistic value*. Is it surprising that the Net Geners prefer personal recommendations to brands or special offers? Information overload tends to confuse more than really help us to make a decision. Why do you think cell phone tariffs from various companies are so incompatible with each other, and almost impossible to evaluate, unless you plan each and every phone call? But here is the crux of the matter: in a downturn lots of these ivory towers are crumbling. *There are opportunities out there to actually negotiate again!* Inverse marketing will help you to reacquaint yourself with this art and accept that everything should be and is negotiable. Proper negotiation should not be a dirty word, nor should it be a "split the difference" attitude. Proper negotiations involve the whole package, from delivery terms to delivery methods, frequency, buffer stocks, quality, payment terms, and so forth.

DON'T BUY TWICE AT THE SHARP END

From inverse marketing we take a big leap to the subject of acquiring another company. The principle of "don't buy twice, but buy wise" applies equally well. There is no doubt that in a severe downturn there are opportunities for the cash rich, and for those who can still convince their banks to provide finance to acquire companies that are hurting or even companies that are basket cases for very reasonable prices. So do we jump in and gobble them up, or do we take some time to consider?

Research Your Potential Acquisition

First of all, remind yourself of the fact that, *regrettably, most acquisitions end up being unsuccessful* for a pretty common reason. This reason is, time and time again, that operational problems are underestimated or even ignored. When we get ourselves to the mental state where we want something, we tend to overlook all the negatives. We have all experienced this on a personal level by buying something we had our mind set on, but after we acquired, it we quickly lost all interest. Ego-driven senior management is no different. At one stage or other, "want to have" takes over from "why do we want this one?" during an acquisition phase. Thus in general most takeovers are not successful; too much is paid for acquisitions, predicted savings of the new enlarged entity are overestimated, balance sheets are overburdened by debt, but above all else, operational problems are ignored. But if you still feel that you can beat the odds and be impartial and clinical—there's nothing wrong with that, I might add—proceed by all means.

Then really concentrate on the intended takeover target. Ask yourself the question, "Why is it for sale?" Continue on with, "What do we know about our intended target?" And follow up with, "What can we find out?" The more you can find out about your intended target, the better. Don't stop at the financial stuff. As you knew or know by now, accounting concepts are just concepts. Past performance expressed in income statements and balance sheets is pretty useless stuff if you don't know what's in the "kitty" now, what current and forecasted sales numbers are, what's really hidden in the debtor and creditor ledgers, what value *you* estimate their stock at, what their management expertise is, what the skill level of the work force is, what the state of the plant or premises is, what their customers think, and so on and so forth. If you can't find out any of that, and you simply go "by the numbers," you might just be taking on an opportunity that will rapidly become an impossible and unworkable challenge.

Finally, concentrate on your own organization. Is a takeover strategy part of your plan? How are you yourself actually doing? Can you really afford this takeover financially and operationally? How are you going to finance the takeover? How are you going to control it? Who is going to run it for you, or do you leave everything as is? Is your own management team mature enough to take on a remote location? Would the team be in favor, or are you going to have an uphill struggle to convince them? It is getting monotonous, but unfortunately it's in the detail again.

Alas, in most instances during a takeover process, rationality disappears, and emotions take over. That's why the eventual purchase price will probably no longer reflect value for money, but a "must have at all cost" desire. On numerous occasions I have said to entrepreneurs who were keen as mustard to buy a competitor that had fallen on difficult times, *You will be making a down payment now and paying installments for the next ten years.*

The foregoing is all related to taking over a potential candidate in your own market environment. Renewed interest in the principles of vertical integration also forms part of managing yourself through a downturn. The principle can best be explained as follows: If you have trouble with a major supplier, take him over, or, alternatively, if you have problems with a major customer, take him over! Although the temptation might be there, the urge should be resisted strongly. They are different businesses from yours, and your management probably knows little about them. So how can you make something work that is outside your area of expertise and needs to improve dramatically? If you can answer that question enthusiastically and substantially, you might be in with a small chance. If not, stay well clear, and concentrate on your own business and its customers. They offer you by far the best chance of survival.

Bargains Probably Are a Canful of Slimy Challenges

It has been said that there are two types of companies for sale, those that are successful and those that are unsuccessful. The first group has to be bought at a premium and can probably be made only marginally better; the second group falls into the category of "we can improve it." The second group is always the one that is for sale in a downturn. So the questions should really be, how do you think you can improve it? Do you have the resources, including the human ones, to improve it and—funny enough—does the takeover target want to be improved?[7] The last question has everything to do with the attitudes of the management of the takeover target. Resentment and fear are the most obvious attitudes. Resentment, because nobody likes to get a new "owner" with all the uncertainties associated with it. Fear, because most takeovers lead to redundancies at the senior management level of the business that is being taken over. After all, what is the point in leaving everything unchanged? You are going to improve it, aren't you? So all those takeover deals in the past where the "sitting management" was retained are a bit of a laugh. It's like starting a one-mile dash with a ball and chain around one of your legs. Integrating two companies to achieve the famous two plus two is five scenario is very hard and detailed work, and it probably takes anywhere from a year to five years. So unless you are prepared to put in the effort, and you have the staff to execute a takeover plan, think very carefully.

Practice Makes Perfect 5.3
Acquisitions and Egos

The time frame for this example of management ego that takes over where common sense left off is not really important. Similar examples of failed acquisitions abound, witness Mercedes Benz and Chrysler, BMW and Rover, and many more in almost all industries.

I was asked to be part of a takeover team by the CEO of a very large public retail company. The acquisition target, let's call it, ACK stores, was a similar but much smaller retailer, a private family company, with close to 75 stores countrywide. After having studied the acquisition target in detail by looking at all the available numbers, visiting the various stores incognito, and getting a feel for their merchandise approach, we submitted our report to the CEO. We valued the potential acquisition in a range of $2.75 to $3.50 per ordinary share. He pegged his initial offer at $2.95 per share. We had our foot in the door.

Negotiations were started. The takeover team was allowed some access to confidential information, and we also visited the acquisition target's head office and a good cross section of their stores in a lot more detail. About 14 days into this exercise, it became known that our biggest competitor was showing interest in ACK stores as well. What ensued was quite frightening. In a two-headed race that can be described only as the ultimate ego trip, the offer price went up from $2.95 to $3.50 to $4.50 to $4.99 per share. Then our final offer was made at \$5.15. When our competitors made a final offer of \$5.19 our final, final offer went up to \$5.25. The leader of our little team had countless discussions with the CEO to warn him that inventory figures appeared to be highly inflated, their staff-to-floor space ratio was twice as large as ours, their head office was bloated with plenty of cousins, nieces, nephews, and friends, their stock turn was atrocious, and so forth. The advice our team leader gave the CEO was to pull out and give the headache to our competitor, who might pull out too. We could then "mop up" in a year or so. But as you guessed, the game went on. Eventually our CEO declared victory at \$5.32 per share.

After the celebrations, our worst fears were confirmed. A year later, only five stores, suitably renamed, remained of the former ACK chain, in towns where we had no stores. Sometimes I still wonder what it would have cost to open five new stores in these towns and watch the demise of ACK from the sidelines.

After the takeover celebrations are over, be prepared to be surprised—surprised by just about everything from top to bottom, left to right, and debit to credit. Also your efforts are going to be resented by employees who do know the business, even if they were not very capable of running it. Don't waste time. *First of all, come to grips with the client base of your acquisition.* If you lose them you are really giving yourself a canful of challenges. Visit your new customers, find out what they liked and what they didn't like, and then make sure it's business as usual—and try to improve quickly. The in-all-probability "allowed benefit" of ownership change by customers tends to be a very small window, so make use of it. Move in your own people at critical junctures and start finding out what is going on. If you want to integrate some parts of the new business with your own, let management think it through very carefully before you implement. If the new business is bleeding, stop the bleeding very quickly; if you don't, blood will start gushing due to the takeover blues.

Do You Really Want the Hassle?

Before you actually make a final decision to proceed with an acquisition, sit back and ask yourself the question again: do we really need this? Sometimes it is much better to let a competitor triumph and let him struggle with sorting out that acquisition you so desperately wanted. In the meantime, you can concentrate on mopping up the customers who are sick and tired of dealing with your competitor or his recent acquisition. He will be fully occupied for the foreseeable future with all those important and juicy "black box" problems that leave customers stone cold. Therefore, for you, walking away from the acquisition is perhaps a much better opportunity. Acquisition of customers from a potential takeover target is a pretty elegant solution compared to the hassle and potential difficulties of integrating and finding the synergy in two different companies, even if they are in the same business and produce similar products.

Gut Feel and Team Input

The graveyard of corporate takeover fans is littered with entrepreneurs and executives who had a "gut feeling" that this potential takeover was the one! Even a gut feeling should be based on something. If gut feeling is based on street-smart thinking, acquired over years and years of practice, then your gut feeling might be worth something. But even then it is important to get your team on board. They are the ones who are going to have to make this work. Don't overestimate your own powers of conviction and underestimate their powers of unspoken doubt. Nobody wants to be the spoilsport of the boss's pet project. It's your job to make sure that they voice their objections sincerely, even if you have to pull these objections out of their heads one at a time! Then you can discuss and seek solutions if there are any. The real cost of a takeover is almost always underestimated. In general terms, there are no real bargains out there—just challenges to be evaluated and then to be faced.

The Grass Is Greener. . . .

If as an organization you have already ventured into foreign parts, you probably know that every new acquisition in a country where your organization has no experience is a test. You have to break down language and cultural barriers, fulfill legal requirements, introduce basic reporting mechanisms, face initial integration problems, and in the process find out what you have really bought. Otherwise the benefit from purchasing power, marketing clout, and all the other clouts that still have to prove themselves will soon turn to overwhelming challenges.[8]

If you haven't had that experience up till now, and you are tempted to go abroad because you have a better change of sitting out a downturn, please don't. A downturn is difficult enough as it is without getting involved in language and cultural barriers. Opportunities in other countries are difficult to evaluate at the best of times. I've sat in meetings where the accountants from both parties had to rely on an accounts clerk, who spoke a language vaguely familiar to both parties, to communicate. That's where you find yourself in those infamous situations where someone in one party appears to speak heatedly for five minutes. Then you, in the other party, ask the translator anxiously, "What did she say?" And the translator says, "she says no." Or even worse, you have tried to make a sincere point; the translator translates, then all the participants on the other side burst out in laughter!

In a downturn, don't even try taking over a foreign company unless you know exactly what you are doing. All this leads to a number of conclusions, namely, *opportunity number 3 is that there are plenty of potential takeover candidates in a downturn; make sure you select the right one!*

But the next opportunity is often much more exciting, namely, *opportunity number 4, mopping up the customers of a struggling competitor is painless compared to taking over the competitor.*

DIFFERENTIATE AND INNOVATE

You can get a lot of mileage out of the interrelated concepts of differentiation and innovation. It's not as easy as it sounds, but it is not impossible either. Those famous and well-published breakthroughs in really novel products during a downturn are one in a million. But, if you have nothing to lose, and you have the idea, now is the time to start that audacious new venture. Supposedly, venture capitalists love those new bold ideas so make it big enough, and you will get the finance! That's the fairy tale come true. Also, you often hear that great entrepreneurs spot a trend before it is obvious. My own take on this is that everyone will interpret and write about that after the idea or trend has proved to be successful. Then it suddenly becomes logical and visionary. Great visions and sound strategies are in the main developed over time, and, lest we forget, outsiders certainly won't be able to help you develop a vision or a strategy. Intimate knowledge of a company's capabilities and the dreams and vision, determination, and hard work of the owners cannot be gleaned and put in a box labeled, "let's set the strategy." For most of us in the existing business world, forget those visions of grandeur and concentrate on incremental improvement before you take a real risky plunge. True enough, a lot of little improvements might even lead you to that really significant breakthrough.

Differentiate and Differentiate Again

Differentiation of a product or a service can be a very effective way to create additional value for customers. Don't think only of the product itself, but of everything associated with the product that will create value or even perceived value for your customers. For example, in a production setting some time ago we found it difficult to match our own production schedule with that of our main customers. We had no extra room to create a buffer stock, and those particular customers didn't want to take on more inventory to solve what they considered was our problem. Endless last-minute production scheduling changes with the associated increase in setup times did not really help the cost and the quality of the end product. We delivered with our own fleet of trucks. Not far from us was a transport company that appeared to have a pretty large facility. In our discussions with them they agreed to manage and store our buffer stock, if we would use their transport services. The numbers worked out similar to our own costs, excluding invisible benefits, such as improved setup times and reduced rejects. We had to improve packaging—more handling often requires better protection for the product—which was an increase in cost; so was additional storage, but all in all, it ended up about cost neutral. With our own production schedule more predictable, the quality improved markedly, manufacturing costs came down, and all those little benefits were the direct result of a not-so-obvious solution by the team that had precious little to do with the product itself.

Differentiate the Physical Package

Packaging is another area where a small change can mean a lot. You can differentiate by size, material, different dispensing, introducing an integral carrying method, resealing possibilities, and so forth. If you go to a supermarket, just observe how inventive manufacturers have become to make their products more visible, more accessible, easier to carry, and more convenient to dispense. That is not even considering the matters unseen by the end consumer, for instance, the superstore distribution center demands for standard dimensions to facilitate handling and storage. Consider in particular the purpose the packaging serves and how long the product is going to be in its packaging. Just because the packaging serves only as protection doesn't mean it is not important. Find out what it looks like in your client's warehouse. If it looks good and solid, you have passed first impressions. If it stacks well in bundles of 10 but not in bundles of 20, but bundles of 10 are too expensive to pack and ship, try to figure out with different packaging materials and perhaps configurations how you can make it stack well in bundles of 20.

Physical packaging is only one aspect of the total package. There are plenty of ways in which you can differentiate the total package without changing the physical characteristics or the delivery. Keep on reminding yourself that value is in the mind, and seek ways and means to utilize this concept. Listen to the remarks made by customers and potential customers. That also means that you must not have rigid ideas in your own mind. Sometimes an innocent remark by a customer, or by a member of your team, might indicate that a slightly different approach is much more suitable that the one you were advocating. Sometimes a subtle difference might make a product suitable for a different market without substantially altering the physical product. *Observe, listen, learn, test, implement, and improve.*

Practice Makes Perfect 5.4
The Keep-the-Couch-Clean Snack Pack

The product was peanuts, roasted in the shell. Bought raw, they were roasted in the shell in a hot-air oven fed by a conveyor belt. Then a cool-air fan, part of the same conveyor, cooled the nuts down. The roasted, cooled peanuts were then fed to a packaging line for weighing and packaging. They were normally sold by us and the competition in packs of about half a kilo, or sometimes even a kilo. It was a pretty popular and well-known product in our extensive snacks-from-nature line. There wasn't a great margin, but this was a solid volume product that complemented our total product line. One of the major retailers who stocked part of our line of snack products had offered us about two square feet at the end of their pretty prominent snack aisle to promote our products for about a month. We were looking for something special, rather than the habitual "buy three, get one free" angle. Also we were overexposed in whole peanuts and could do with a bit of a clearance sale. My team came up with the idea of packaging the product in a cheap, round plastic container about 8 inches in diameter and about 4 inches tall. The lid fit snugly over the top of the container, but was itself 3.5 inches deep. The idea was to use the lid for the shells and skins that had to be discarded while you were cracking and peeling the nuts. The circumference of the container was used to advertise the product and explain what the lid was for by means of a printed paper strip glued to the inside. For those of you who have never had a do-it-yourself snack experience since ready-to-eat snacks have become the norm, eating roasted peanuts from the shell is quite a messy but enjoyable "grazing" business while one is occupied with something really useful, such as watching sports on the tube.

As this special container could not be filled by means of our existing packaging lines, we looked for alternatives. In the end we took on 15 students to package the containers by hand. It was a bit on the expensive side, but it was, after all for a special promotion. The promotion itself was a great success. The containers sold like hotcakes. We kept the special packaging line going well beyond the end of the promotion. Then we had to discontinue because the containers didn't fit that well on the regular shelves.

After-Service as Part of the Overall Product

Obviously, service is a very powerful differentiator and hence value creator. Particularly service that is dispensed by the people in your own organization. It's an extremely powerful weapon that is oh-so-difficult to copy if it's not delivered in a genuine fashion. Make it sincere, and customers will take note. A lot of modern products do not require regular contact with the supplier or retailer. As an organization you might have only one chance to make an impression and leave the customer with a good, neutral, or bad feeling. Make use of this chance and create a ripple effect that goes well beyond the one customer. Word of mouth is very powerful, and so are the modern equivalents such as Facebook, LinkedIn, Twitter, chat sites, and blogs (Not considering the ones we don't even know about yet!).

If a customer comes back because there was something wrong with the product, you have a great second chance to make a lasting impression. Make sure that staff who deal with customer complaints are well prepared for them and, if possible, rotate those staff members frequently and motivate them continually. In a store setting it is not a bad policy to let every salesperson spend one day every week at the customer service counter where you deal with customer queries and complaints.

If the product needs to be serviced from time to time, or if it must be repaired, you have a fantastic chance to develop customer loyalty. Use that opportunity, and make sure the service staff knows that they are part of your total package and sales effort. Teach all service staff basic selling techniques and how to deal with complaints. If you have a recurring chance to be in contact with your customers, use it instead of sending out the monthly or yearly invoice as a stark reminder of bad news. After all, an invoice is seldom good news. Try to make it a little bit more special by adding a newsletter, announcing a new product, and so forth. If you can, and if it is practical, hand-deliver invoices and use the opportunity to find out whether all is well, and your service lives up to its reputation. You are not looking for an earthquake; you are looking for the subtle yet powerful ripple effect that is created by the little stone that is dropped into the lake. You might never even know what the ripple eventually hit, but in time you will benefit because you are practicing real customer satisfaction and retention.

Innovation Is a Real Team Effort

Personally I like to think of innovation as a result of constantly seeking differentiation. That is not to say that certain leaps forward are not possible; every business needs a leap or a jolt sometimes. On the contrary, it is much more likely that what is sometimes referred to as a learning organization will produce an innovation because the whole team is looking for improvements all the time. Real innovation does not happen that often, but if it does, it can create a whole new wave in your company or even in an industry. So give the Net Gener who just came to you with an outrageous idea the time of day, and let him convince you that he really believes in his idea and is prepared to develop it a bit more before you even consider taking it farther. Give him some time to develop the idea, and follow up! Or consider the pensioner who is employed part-time in your packaging department and who is making noises that at company X 20 years ago they did ABC, and that worked much better than what you are doing currently. Listen to him and get him to explain in detail.

The ultimate achievement is for your organization to become what Collins and Porras referred to as a visionary team as opposed to a single visionary.[9] This is particularly difficult to achieve for the growing entrepreneurial organization with often only one visionary leader, the entrepreneur.[10] In larger, more established organizations, it is difficult to imagine that, for example, a machine operator or an insurance clerk needs or wants to feel part of a visionary team. That's why the vision needs to be translated into something simple, consistent, and applicable to different levels of the organization. For the machine operator and the insurance clerk, the vision might be to reduce the number of rejects or to reduce the number of data entry errors, respectively. That is what translation of a vision in an organization means: to explain in a logical way what needs to be done correctly in order to keep a customer happy. The chances that a machine operator will come up with a real innovation are probably one in a million, but if he does, he should know that he can come to you, and then you had better listen carefully! That is what a visionary organization really means and is capable of doing, day in and day out.

Differentiation and innovation are the lifeblood of any organization. But in a downturn they might just make the difference between that which flourishes and that which struggles. *Opportunity number five is to tap your collective knowledge base and seek continuous differentiation; real innovation might be the reward.*

BE A LEADER AND DEVELOP THE TEAM

Great opportunities don't come around too often. A very long period of growth and a well-developed focus on individual importance must lead to a fantastic opportunity in a downturn, namely, the rediscovery of the organization as a team and you as a team leader. Notice there are two elements here—team and team leadership. So a process of change should also address these two elements.

The world abounds with change consultants who have reported that 75% of organizational change programs fail.[11] Why do we keep on listening to these folks when we know that their success rate is so dismal? Unfortunately there is not very much that they can do; their benefactor, the client CEO, wants a change program, but fails to see that she and her top team have to be included. Only a very courageous consultant who is prepared to tell his benefactor that she primarily will have to adjust her behavior will succeed here. Unfortunately there are not many of those around; it's much easier to report that programs fail because they do not attract enough support at the grass-roots level.

Lead by Example

"Lead by example" sounds easy and far too simple. Nevertheless it is the most powerful technique to demonstrate that you are pretty serious about what you want the organization to achieve. If you truly understand and believe in the company's vision, you should be able to teach it, translate it, and practice it yourself. How can you expect employees to take your latest forceful lecture on cost savings seriously if the day after you show up in a brand new executive car? Or sternly lecture that from now on everyone is supposed to be in the office on time, and then you arrive late every day for a week. For you it might be a small point because the car was ordered some time ago, and you work all hours of the day and night anyway. But what is important is the message that is transmitted to everyone else. You can't preach and practice two different things if you want to be a leader. That is why "lead by example" and "respect has to be earned" are very closely associated. You can't get respect if you don't set the example. That is what is required from a team leader: set the norms and lead by example. Improve the world, and start with yourself is applicable in the microenvironment of your own business as well. Only then will you reap the full benefits of team play.

Make It Clear What Has to Be Achieved

The trouble with a lot of soft-skill management stuff is that it all seems to make sense until you have to apply it in real life, in the workplace. That is where experience comes in. There is no quick and dirty substitute for life experience. You can read all you like and attend any number of courses, but if you don't start practicing and gaining experience, you will never pick up the practical skills of management. That is also where the right type of mentor can help, by giving guidance over a period of time. In large organizations it should not be a problem to allocate a suitable mentor to younger managers. In a small organization you might have to look outside. Make sure that you find a mentor who has the necessary skills and, above all, the necessary management experience. After all, it's management experience and practical skills that you are after, not more theory.

If you are somewhat apprehensive about starting to improve your practical management skills, you can perhaps imagine what change will mean to most employees. For employees, all that mumbo jumbo management stuff scares the living daylights out of them, and it certainly does not get them motivated to "get with the program." But how can they get with the program if they don't fully understand it? So it is up to you, the manager, to translate all these wonderful concepts, such as vision, strategy, objectives, and targets into everyday achievable detail. Nobody is trying to prove to anybody how clever we managers are. To achieve a purpose, you have to communicate using the appropriate approach to the level that needs to receive the message. Set the performance targets, and most employees can be left alone to achieve them. The more freedom you can give them in deciding how to achieve the objective, the better it is. Putting their own ideas into practice and providing input that's listened to are very powerful motivators for all employees. Set them free, but retain control, and never compromise on clarity and purpose. So keep communications simple, direct, concise, and consistent. If this is practiced at all levels of an organization, and the details are attended to, you will get it right, no matter what it is that you are trying to achieve.

Practice Makes Perfect 5.5
It's All in the Detail

The CEO of a very large national retail company used to spend one to two days out of every 14 on unannounced store visits. He used to travel by limousine and he was always accompanied by the relevant area management team, consisting of the operations manager, merchandise manager, controller, and personnel manager. I had the privilege to be part of his entourage on several occasions. The drill was always the same: travel time was used to brief him intensely on the personnel in the store, names, recent happenings, personal details, and so forth. On arrival the entourage went straight to the store manager's office to let him know that this was his "lucky day" and to prepare him for what was about to happen, namely, that he would be grilled on all the detail and the numbers. This particular CEO had a photographic memory and could retain numbers and facts from reports and briefings like a plugged-in 32-gigabyte memory stick.

While the team was spending time with the store manager, our CEO went on what the Australians call a *walkabout*. He would look here and would look there, greet every staff member by name, make small talk, ask simple questions, give compliments, and so on. Even the personal detail, only recently acquired during travel time briefings, was never forgotten, such as "Mary, congratulations on passing your driving test," or "Bill, is Kathy out of the hospital yet?" He was even known to give advice to customers such as, "That really looks good on you," or "I would try that in blue, if I were you." This used to take the better part of two hours. Then he would enter the manager's office and grill all of us on the results of this particular store.

He never criticized anyone in a group, and he always observed the chain of command in reprimanding; if the store scored badly, you were told first and then you had to make sure the store manager got to know about it. Among his famous sayings were, "I employ you people to watch the detail; if you can't do it, I'll find someone who can." Or something like, "Don't blame the store manager. If he is that bad, you should have done something about it." Needless to say the floor staff and the customers— quite a few of these knew who he was–absolutely loved him!

Give Continuous Feedback

Nothing is more soul destroying to the average employee than to get no feedback at all. Part of attending to the detail is making sure that you give feedback on a regular basis. If things have gone particularly well, say so. When things have not gone so well, tell them that too, and then offer them support and, if need be, advice. Always listen to what people have to say, but don't let them get away with not doing what has to be achieved. It's in the detail, and if the detail is not going well, then sooner or later the business will suffer. Getting feedback helps employees feel good and even special about what they do. Consistency, attention to detail, and feedback are the cornerstones of developing your team.

Be Decisive When You Have To Be

There are always instances where further consultation must stop, or where there simply is no time for consultation or discussion. Try to get as many facts as possible, and then make your decision. That's "the buck stops here" time. Make your decision, tell everyone concerned what you decided, and then follow through. Be decisive and act decisively. That is also the job of the team leader.

Particularly in difficult times, you can't always consult to the *nth* degree to get everybody on board. That is almost impossible anyway. You might have to resort to a more "command and control" approach. If you do, make sure employees understand that what is being transmitted is not open for discussion or optional. Particularly Net Geners might have to get used to the urgency of this type of situation. Their life to date has not been ruled by "have to do" and "want it now" demands. But most of them are pretty smart and will learn fast. So at every opportunity, talk to them, explain the why to them, help them understand the objective, give them the freedom to achieve it their way—but by your deadline—encourage them, and, if required and relevant, set the example.

Cross-Functional Teams

For specific purposes, for example, for the introduction of a new product, the discontinuation of an unprofitable product, or the closing of a facility it is not uncommon nowadays to form a cross-functional team. A cross-functional team should consist of a group of people from different disciplines, who have a specific task. After the task is completed, the team is disbanded. Such a team should include employees of all levels of an organization. The only consideration should be, can each individual member contribute her knowledge for the specific task? The team should have access to all knowledge that is required for the task, but in very large organizations, that is often compromised by politics and departmental jealousy. A cross-functional team should be formed only for a real single objective. After all, a management team is cross-functional too, but based on the existing hierarchy.

Be very careful with setting up cross-functional teams in difficult times. If such a team is not managed correctly, you will find that a lot of time is wasted and another information-generating stream has to be managed. The idea that cross-functional teams are self-directed and should respond to broad objectives only is a leftover from the good times. In a downturn you can't afford to have a team look at unstructured decisions, such as what markets to compete in, what new production technologies to invest in, or other vague strategic directions. That is the job of management, with the ideas and thoughts that are generated in their own teams.

Cross-functional teams work best in organizations with a well-developed overall team sense. It's another way of asking, if your organization is a good team, who needs cross-functional teams? To introduce cross-functional teams in an organization to compensate for weak management and supervisory teams is just not going to work. Why would a weak, political management team take the advice of a cross-functional team? Get someone such as an interim general manger to shock the management team into action, purge the really weak links, and start developing the operational team on the run.

However, and with due concern for those considerations, for particular and well-defined outcomes, a cross-functional team may very well be the answer. It is important to remember, though, that each member of the team needs his individual tasks well defined. It also helps if the members of the team are passionate about the common objective that has to be achieved.

Bad Practice Makes Perfect 5.6
Cross-Functional Nightmares

In this national subsidiary of a large multinational there were five cross-functional teams in operation to achieve the introduction of what was then called an MRP, or Materials Requirement Planning, system. This MRP system had to be tied into the existing cost accounting system that had been in operation in all subsidiaries for about a year. In addition to keeping track of raw materials and the end product, the individual ingredients that went into each end product had to be traceable as well. This particular subsidiary served the national market, but it also had production facilities and a warehouse to serve the continent. For this MRP project there were consultants involved on each team. Apart from consultants from the software provider, there were management consultants as well, because the end result might well mean an adjustment to the organization. Also there were representatives from finance, production, logistics, systems, marketing and even the personnel department. When I got involved in this, I had recently joined this subsidiary in a line function; I was made the head of Project Group III as well, "Integration of MRP with Cost Control." The previous leader of Project Group III had left the organization. The project groups met at least twice a week to discuss progress and address issues of integration between the project groups. The leaders of the five groups then met once a week to try to resolve these issues. All in all, this required a pretty heavy time commitment in addition to a pretty demanding line function. But I was young and very eager.

Particularly the management consultants kept these project groups going. They had appointed themselves as secretaries to each project group. Reams of paper and diagrams were produced, minutes of meetings, agenda points and reports for next meetings, endless discussions on what could perhaps happen and what could then conceivably be done, functional upgrades, requirement changes, diagram additions and deletions—you name it, and it was being discussed and, what is more, painstakingly documented. I got pretty sick of it pretty soon and decided to seek some solution. In talking to the logistics manager I discovered that what had started as a pretty straightforward exercise a year earlier had turned into a political monster driven by the management consultants who were brought on board by the regional production VP.

So the two of us decided to find out what the production manager had to say. When he discovered what our feelings were, he really let it rip. Apparently this had all been set up over his head to make a political point, in his words. Unfortunately, the general manager was not in the least interested. As long as his local sales figures met budget, he couldn't care less about regional warehousing and cost accounting. The personnel manager was not interested either. He had a pretty large staff and a couple of people dedicated to the project team. He was happy enough. The systems manager was equally unconcerned. He was the proud manager of double the number of staff that he had had before the project was started. It all counts in job evaluation systems you know. Eventually we found an ally in the regional senior VP. He started to ask some awkward questions, pulled the expense out of the budget, and the whole project was shelved. The regional Production VP was moved back to the States, and the consultants submitted their last invoices. The project filing cabinets were moved to storage, and peace returned. Later on we found that there already was a head office team in the United States that was studying the integration of the cost accounting system with another MRP package.

Virtual Teams

One of the latest trends made feasible by ever-more-efficient communication technologies is the notion of virtual teams. The belief that people need to meet every day to get their work done and need the discipline of an office environment might not always be true. When people have the opportunity to work on engaging, well-planned tasks at home, they have been shown to be significantly more productive and committed than those who struggle with commuter traffic every day. The operative word here is no doubt *well-planned*. In essence, this smacks of a very strict regime, where certain tasks have to be completed by certain deadlines in order to serve the whole. What has changed? To me this is more like a situation of command and control by remote control. How far this new "old" idea can and will be practiced will no doubt depend on the task at hand. Routine office tasks might lend themselves to this type of virtual team, and so might high-powered teams that consist of self-motivating experts seeking a solution to a particular problem. The questions remain: how are teams like that managed and controlled, and will this type of virtual team further deteriorate real interactive management skills? Time will tell. Virtual teams might be a solution to some situations, but management responsibility remains as is.

Empower Talented People

Within the structure of the overall team it is also important to set really talented people free. Give them the special assignments, watch how they break down the departmental barriers, how they get the information by hook or by crook, and achieve what you asked them to do in record time, often on their own! Talented people are either genuine functional experts or very ambitious young managers. They are part of the real future of the company. Spend time with them, challenge them continuously, teach them, council them, but above all set them free. A lot of older managers might not be too familiar with the latest developments on the Internet and how it can be used to generate more sales, better exposure, and so forth. Listen to the talented Net Geners, let them teach you, let them convince you, and then make up your mind about what to do. As a manager you should never be too old to learn and develop yourself, and in the process help really talented people develop the skills they don't have.

Reap the Benefits

The beauty of sound team development is that you are no longer alone, and you can rely on the combined know-how and effort of the team. You can start challenging team members and expect more and more from them. For me, many a first-rate solution has developed in the past because I said to the team, "There must be a better or cheaper way of doing this." The very best opportunities are created by your own organization, as long as it learns to listen to itself. So listen to everyone, particularly to those employees who are in contact with customers on a daily basis; don't be led by employees, but listen intently. They know a lot more than you think. A lot of what you will hear is probably "noise," but it is very much a part of your job to filter the noise from the good stuff.

When your team starts to practice attending to the detail in their own teams, you will soon start noticing changes. The real challenge here is to be consistent and just keep plugging away. You can't relax for one moment. That is why running a company or a department is hard, but satisfying work. My own conviction is that if you start with yourself, you can achieve anything with your team, and you will never need extravagant change programs that end up having a 75% chance of not succeeding. As a team manager you don't need to be the most inventive of the team at all. What you do need to be is the encourager and stimulator of ever-increasing improvement thinking, the occasional leap forward, and the guardian of the vision. Now you are really starting to earn your keep!

A well-functioning team is the direct opposite of the self-centered culture so prevalent after a prolonged boom period. Even the Net Geners and the former "knowledge workers" must get used to the idea that "brand me," the search for meaning, and other vague ideas have to be put on hold, during hours of paid employment anyway. Instead of those, a well-functioning team and attention to detail will provide the best chance of coming out of a downturn in much better shape than the organization was in going into it. *Opportunity number six is to develop your team and your own team leadership and reap the benefits.*

TEACH YOURSELF TO LISTEN AND OBSERVE ACTIVELY

Active listening, sometimes referred to as aggressive listening, is not an easy skill to acquire for most managers, including me. Listening is such a natural habit that putting some effort into it doesn't seem to make a lot of sense. Active listening is pretty challenging because most people are much more focused on what they are saying and what they want to say or are going to say than on what they are hearing in return. Sending is perceived as more important by most of us than receiving. Voice mails and e-mails are no exception. The sender thinks that his message is urgent, helpful, and fully worthy of the receiver's attention, but the receiver disagrees. The ability to listen to what someone is actually saying is probably one of the greatest assets that we can develop.

Actively observing is a close second. People are forever expressing themselves in ways that will go unnoticed unless you are keenly aware and notice them. Observing actively means that you are trying to get the overall picture, taking all the intentional and unintentional signals, and converting them into useful perceptions. So let us dive a bit deeper into the art of active listening and observing, another "soft management skill" that is as hard as well-cured premium concrete if you learn to use it and then force yourself to start practicing it. To practice it you can use a number of helpful techniques, namely,

- Concentrate on what the other party is saying.
- Try to avoid early assessments.

- Convey in a nonverbal way that you are listening.
- Ask questions and paraphrase.
- Notice how the message is conveyed.
- Use "the pregnant pause."
- Avoid getting defensive.
- Note your own talk/listen ratio.
- Observe.

Let's explore all of these in a bit more detail.

Concentrate on What the Other Party Is Saying

How often have you found your thoughts drifting while listening to someone talking to you? If there is something else on your mind, like a report that needs to be finished, an upcoming press interview, or a pressing family matter, you might not have heard a word of what the other person is saying. Or perhaps you are already thinking of what to ask next or the next point that you want to make, and you miss some vital points in the current conversation. We do it all the time, and therefore we really need to concentrate on what is being said.

Try to Avoid Early Assessments

How many times have you already made a judgment about what is being said before the speaker is finished? Or how often have you already assumed or guessed what the speaker is going to say next? Unfortunately, the fact that we can listen at a faster rate than the rate at which most people talk leads us easily to the tendency of arriving at early conclusions.[12] It requires a conscious effort to keep listening and not jump to conclusions.

Convey in a Nonverbal Way That You Are Listening

The best way of showing that you are listening is keeping eye contact at all times when someone is talking. Do you acknowledge what is being said by nodding your head, are you leaning forward and not using your hands to draw pictures or play with a pencil or modify a paperclip? In other words, does your body language confirm that you are listening? The common notion among communication experts is that nonverbal messages are three times as powerful as verbal ones. Convey the message that you are not listening, and effective communication will break down very quickly. If you are the speaker, and you note behavior like that, you'd better do something. How many times have we sat through a presentation where the sales person just plodded on regardless while his audience was doing anything but listen?

Ask Questions and Paraphrase

It is a very powerful technique to ask clarification of what you have just heard. For example, "So if I hear you correctly, you want us to consider giving your company a discount of 3% for the next shipment?" If possible ask open-ended questions to clarify points or to obtain additional information. You could follow up by asking, "Is there any particular reason for that?" Don't make the question sound as if you have already made up your mind. You are after more and better information, not final judgment as yet.

Paraphrasing can also be used effectively to convey the message that you are listening actively. For example, a client might say, "I have been unfairly treated because the day after I bought my widget, prices came down by 10%. I am a regular customer, and it doesn't feel right." Then you might paraphrase by saying, "I can see that you, as a regular customer, are upset and feel that you have been unfairly treated by our latest discount offer on widgets." Paraphrasing is a very powerful technique to improve your listening skills. First, you need to listen very well so you can paraphrase correctly, and second, you are indicating to the sender that the message was received correctly. As a bonus, it often takes the sting out of an accusation or a "you are to blame" or "can't you see I'm upset" speech.

Bad Practice Makes Perfect 5.7
Jumping to Conclusions

Scene: Late 1970s, at an exhibition in England where the company I was representing had an exhibition booth. Two gentlemen had just entered this stand. I had noticed that they were speaking German to each other, and, being proud of the fact that I can speak that language, I addressed them in German. We had an animated conversation about our products and their use until I asked the question, "What part of Germany are you from?" One of them looked at me with a pained expression and said, "Actually we are from Switzerland." (In my defense, there are big differences in German dialects, never mind about Swiss German.) They walked off leaving me feeling an inch tall and ready to shrink even farther.

It had been quite a first week as interim general manager, trying to bring some order into what was quite a shambles, in my eyes anyway.

As usual I adopted an open-door policy, and I had been visited almost continually by employees; all of them without exception were after a pay raise. Apparently no one had had an increase for over five years. There's consistency for you! So now it was almost five o'clock on a Monday afternoon, and I was looking forward to a quiet evening. Into my office barged one of the factory workers. He closed the door and asked, "A word please, sir?"

Without hesitation I retorted, "And how much are you looking for?" He looked at me with a puzzled expression and answered, "I don't know what you are talking about, but I want to show you something." He continued, "These parts [showing me a broken widget] we are getting from ABC are real rubbish; they keep on breaking off."

Notice How the Message Is Put Across

Concentrate not only on what is said, but on how it is said. In other words, actively observe; notice how the speaker is standing, the tone of voice, and so forth. If a person raises her voice, she is probably angry or frustrated. Looking down may be interpreted as being shy or embarrassed; an inappropriate silence may be a sign of aggression or an intended punishment; but leaning forward and making eye contact tends to exhibit confidence.

Use the Pregnant Pause

Sometimes when someone has made a statement or has answered a question, you might just try saying nothing: just nod and keep eye contact. Seven times out of ten, the other person will break this pregnant silence and give more information—sometimes even unasked for information—explain her point in a different way, or elaborate. The reason for this is that silence can often be experienced as uncomfortable: hence the automatic reaction to try to break it. However, don't let a pregnant pause end up in a silence contest either. There is a fine line between a pregnant pause and an expected reaction.

Avoid Getting Defensive

It is easy enough to get angry or upset because what you appear to be hearing does not agree with you. Active listening does not mean that you have to agree with what is being said, but it does mean that you are prepared to listen to what is being said. If too much time is spent explaining, elaborating, or defending your decision or your position, it is a sure sign that you are not listening. That is because your role has changed from listener to that of a person convincing others that they are wrong. After listening to a suggestion you do not subscribe to, you could respond by saying, "I understand your point. We just disagree on this one." Active listening also means to listen calmly, even when someone is offering unjust criticism.

Note Your Own Talk-Listen Ratio

Everyone can talk less, and most of us should definitely be talking a hell of a lot less. By talking less, you will hear more, learn plenty, and see things you would not have seen. Consequently you will frequently end up making fewer mistakes. Don't ask questions and then begin to answer them yourself. Note your own talk-listen ratio. By keeping a mental score of this ratio, you might first of all realize that you, yes you, also fall into the most common of groups—the talkers—even though you aspire to become a more balanced talker-listener. It is not easy, but the rewards of active listening are infinitely more rewarding than the effort you have to put in.

Observe

People continuously make statements about themselves, both consciously and unconsciously. Most conscious statements are quite visual, such as the way people dress, the way they carry themselves, and lots of other subtle or brash ways in which people are trying to create an impression. What we are after in a business situation is to go after the overall picture, based on what you see and hear. It could be compared with establishing a comfort zone, or, if you like, the boundaries you need to observe to deal most effectively with a particular person. The most significant and revealing object for observation must be the eyes. Eyes will often tell you more than anything else what someone is really thinking, even when all the other signs are pointing elsewhere. Remember, when people can't use words, they communicate with their eyes. When you are in a meeting with more than one person, watch them make eye contact with each other. It will help you decide what they are really thinking, and indicate who the real decision maker is. That could be critical. It might not be the one with the most impressive title on his business card! Sometimes the listener's eyes will tell you whether you are boring him to tears, and you must think seriously of a radical switch in your current approach or presentation.

At this stage you might well ask yourself, why is all this so important for managing when times are tough? The answer is really very straightforward. In good times when customers want your products, most of us start thinking that we are really pretty good at what we are doing. Then the downturn comes around. Suddenly customers become more demanding, are bombarded by special offers, get visits from competitors' salespersons, and start asking awkward questions. Suddenly we find ourselves in a different world. We might have heard of active listening and observing, but who cares? Products almost sold themselves as long as there was stock. Superficiality reigned supreme! No need to practice all these soft skills; you don't really need them. Thus, the real opportunity is to start practicing these well-known but perhaps forgotten skills and create the edge. If you can create the edge in any situation that requires face-to-face interaction or negotiation, you can help your business through difficult times. *Opportunity number seven is that active listening and observing are incredibly powerful, real value-adding skills, particularly in difficult situations.*

COMMUNICATE HONESTLY: A REAL OPPORTUNITY

Communication in, for, and about an organization has always been an essential part of the business environment. Good or bad publicity can have an effect, not only on the share price, but on the morale of employees and on the perception of customers. Thus communication needs to be treated as a powerful weapon. The moment you issue a staff bulletin, you are not only addressing your staff, but everyone in the wider world who cares to pay attention. Recently there have been a number of examples of careless use of words or opinions in e-mails and SMS text messages that got senior managers of very large corporations into big trouble.[13] Far too many people are treating modern methods of communication in a flippant and off-handed manner until it is too late. Unfortunately these methods are much easier to trace and to recover than their old-fashioned equivalents, the letter and the fax. Just do not be careless, and treat all forms of communication with respect.

In essence there is no difference between internal and external communications. The message might be different, and so might be the purpose, but the audience is very hard to control. Don't even try. Make sure that the message is consistent. For example, don't say in an investment briefing that you are contemplating closing Factory X, and then tell employees that there will be no redundancies in the foreseeable future. Both messages might be correct; you might have advanced plans to offer staff at Factory X voluntary redundancy or positions in other plants, but the damage is done. Your employees will feel betrayed and will demand to know exactly what is going on. You will have lost the initiative and are now in full retreat, trying to defend yourself and regain confidence. In difficult times, communication takes on a critical role; thus it is important to reinforce some basic tenets for managers at all levels in your organization.

The Essentials

Be a leader. You don't have to have all the answers, but tell your team what you know and what you don't know. Tell them what is happening and what the organization is doing to address the unfavorable situation. Be extremely visible. Don't hide in your office. Increase your visits to the factory floor and other places of work, talk to people, and keep on reiterating what the company's core competencies and values are. Explain how these competencies will help the company face the difficulties in the marketplace and also how they will make the company prosper again in the future. Use your management team to convey this message. Make sure it is consistent. Let no manager be a bystander. Be discreet, and reinforce this so your managers are discreet. Make your managers aware of the potential danger of employees overhearing informal discussions that tend to sweep through an organization like a brushfire. Once the damage is done, it's done.

Don't try to practice message control. Find out what the feeling is on the factory floor and what is on employees' minds; have a system in place to quickly answer any potentially damaging messages that appear in the local or national press, on blog or chat sites and the like. Quickly react formally to rumors or inaccurate statements and squash them before they take root. *But here is the basic principle that must overshadow all basics: keep on repetitively reinforcing customer focus.* That surely should always remain the essence of communication, even in difficult times.

Communicate Job Losses

Serious downturns always involve job losses. We discussed this already in Chapter 4 under "Savings Must Be Found." When all the other cost-control measures are not sufficient, then job losses are inevitable. This is a sad fact, but unfortunately true. The process of making people redundant can be potentially very damaging to an organization, so there should be a well-controlled communication plan in place to cater to this unhappy task. If you have the resources, put a small project team together; if not, you will have to do it all by yourself. The plan should be based on the following principles:

- Communicate all the time to your staff. If you don't communicate, the grapevine and rumors will take over so quickly that you won't realize what hit you. As long as you are still planning the process, focus their attention on customer service.

- Always be honest and open. Don't beat about the bush, but don't create unrealistic expectations either. There are plenty of indications for the troops that something is afoot. Even an increase in management meetings and closed doors can be an indication to them that something is about to happen.
- At all times use simple language that can be understood by the population it is meant for; never hide behind legal terms or management jargon.
- Carefully choose the day and time for the start of the redundancy program. Always inform the unfortunate victims before anyone else. Deal with the matter as the labor laws in your environment dictate. In preference, let the unfortunates leave immediately. Anyone who is made redundant and who has to be around will feel unwanted, unvalued, depressed, angry, or cynical—not necessarily in that order. Employees who have been let go might voice these emotions to those around them and knowingly or unknowingly poison the working atmosphere. So think carefully before you allow employees to work after their notice. Inform the survivors and outsiders, such as customers, suppliers, trade organizations, and the press. If you can't contact them all yourself, decide who will do what and how. Issue a statement if you think it will be necessary. If you are approached by the press, never say "no comment." Stick to the statement and give them no additional information. If there is additional information, your staff should hear it first!
- After this bad news has been absorbed, you should use any type of good news to start building internal morale and external confidence. This is always a very difficult one. You can't be too upbeat, because then it increases the feeling of *was it all really necessary?* But you really need to find some positive news among all the doom and gloom. Dig, and you will find it!
- Keep on communicating. Don't stop now; the survivors will be badly shaken too. Everyone will speculate, will there be a next round? And who will be next? Don't promise anything you can't do; be honest, and communicate what you do know.

When the unfortunate victims have left, the workplace will be different for the survivors. Mixed feelings are part of the survivors' emotions; relief that they retained their jobs and a strange feeling of loss for their ex-colleagues. Empty desks, quiet offices, and abandoned machines remind everyone of the stark unfortunate reality of the situation. The best way to get over that quickly and regain momentum is by giving direction.

Practice Makes Perfect 5.8
The Case against Working after Being Given Notice

Opinions vary on how to deal with notice periods when staff are made redundant. Do they work after being given notice, or do you just escort them off the premises when you have given notice? Personally, I'm a firm believer in immediate action and facing the consequences of the action afterward. The underlying motives are based on the concept that "you can make them stay, but you can't make them work," and "don't live in the past; get on with it and shape the future."

A most extreme case of prolonging the agony occurred in the 1990s when I was asked to take over as interim general manager for a company that was balancing on the brink of total failure. The owners, who had not been active in the company for quite some time, had insisted that the previous general manager, let's call him Mr. Knave or MK for short, worked out his notice period, a splendid six months. The owners felt very bitter about his performance, but they were terribly scared that sales would collapse if MK left. MK had had the run of the place for about five years without much control from the directors, but that is another story. I tried to convince the directors that it might just be better to swallow, pay the six months, and move on, but they wouldn't budge.

In the first month I did get a bit of information out of MK, but he spent an inordinate amount of time with a couple of salesmen, drank a lot of coffee, and read a lot of trade magazines. He wasn't particularly bitter about his termination, but he obviously didn't think much of the directors. It's difficult to control someone who falls outside your chain of control, is under a death sentence, and holds a grudge. To me it was pretty clear that he was trying to get his own show off the ground with a couple of the salesmen while he was still being subsidized by his current employer. There were plenty of problems in production, logistics, and the office, but I decided to give this hunch a bit of priority.

I started to visit customers and started fishing. After a couple of weeks of visits I bagged the big one. A customer really opened up and told me that he had been approached by MK, all right. MK had told him that the company was going bust, but said that he had convinced the sales force to leave with him and start anew. Apparently he had it all worked out. The factory foreman was part of the plot also. Keeping this to myself for the time being, I started to keep an eye on MK with great care and to observe his comings and goings. He wasn't doing anything much apart from calling customers and holding endless discussions with some of the salesmen.

After another month and more evidence of my suspicion, I decided to break the news to the owners. They were aghast and furious and wanted to sue the man for every penny he had. There's not much point in that approach if you have scant proof of malpractice. And it's not very clever to ask your clients to testify to your own company's incompetence. Fortunately, they started to listen to me and played it my way. MK was let go with immediate effect and given his full notice pay. I did explain the situation to MK, and I told him that we were considering charges of fraud. Then I hauled in all the salesmen and the factory foreman one by one and told them that I knew about their "dirty little plot." They could choose—get on with the job and help the company recover lost ground, or I would fire them, inform our clients and the industry federation, and they would have to take their chances with a court case. Not one of them chose the latter option. It also materialized that MK had done business for himself by skimming off some of the profits and dealing on the side with our stock, and even with stock that he had purchased on his own and stored in our warehouse! It was a business within a business. Once we got to the bottom of it all, we had a fighting chance!

Postredundancy Direction Reinforced

Once the unpleasantness of the actual redundancy announcement has been made, you need to immediately take control and direct the survivors. More than likely, additional workloads have to be discussed, duties of those who left must be reallocated, shifts need to be realigned, machines have to be mothballed, sales areas get adjusted, and so forth. All these changes should have been prepared in detail, but now the planning phase is over, and you are operating in real time. Real time can throw the best of plans into disarray, and that is where experience comes in again. So discuss the changes, listen to the reactions, and deal with the concerns. There are bound to be details that have not been considered by you and the planners. So the next couple of days or weeks are going to be extra intensive to make sure that all, and I mean all, the detail will still be attended to. If you keep everyone busy and committed, morale can be repaired quite quickly. Reinforce why the redundancies were necessary against the overall plan and where the company needs to be. Often employees may convey negativity and cynicism in difficult times, but most of them are really looking for something to believe in. Make them believe in the goals and the mission and the importance of attending to the detail. All this will help to make the team recover quickly, fit to fight another day.

Customer Communication: Business as Usual

It obviously depends on what type of business you have and how close your customers were to some of the employees who are no longer there. The smaller the organization, the more customers will notice immediately that their contact has been removed abruptly. It might be necessary, if it is practical of course, to visit customers and introduce them to the new contact person. Chances are that your customers, who tend to operate in the same industry or marketplace, are well aware of difficult trading conditions. Don't explain why you did what you did, just concentrate on the good news: it's business as usual for them, you will make sure of that. Remind yourself that, when all is said and done, customers will be product focused; they don't really care what happens in your black box as long as the service does not suffer. It is also an ideal opportunity to face your customers and get some up-to-date intelligence on how they are doing. If the downturn is severe enough, they must be hurting too, and the more you know the better you can keep on serving them. It's all about creating confidence and continuity.

Strategy theory tells us that every weakness is strength, and every problem is an opportunity. *Opportunity number eight is to communicate to customers that it is business as usual, and prove it!*

The Opportunities Summarized

1. Filter out the noise, but be very well informed so you can use developing trends or sentiments to your benefit.
2. Apply inverse marketing to support marketing.
3. There are plenty of potential takeover candidates in a downturn; make sure you select the right one!
4. Mopping up the customers of a struggling competitor is painless compared to a takeover of that competitor.
5. Tap your collective knowledge base and seek continuous differentiation; innovation might be the reward.
6. Develop your team and your own team leadership, and reap the benefits.
7. Active listening and observing are incredibly powerful, real value-adding skills, particularly in difficult situations.
8. Communicate to customers that it is business as usual, and prove it!
9. The *detail*, always the *detail*.

CHAPTER 6

NO TIME TO WASTE

Sometimes it is not enough to do our best; we must do what is required.
—*Winston Churchill (1874–1965)*

There is a pretty well-known financial concept called *earnings before interest and tax,* EBIT for short, that forms part of the management vocabulary. I am going to use the same expression (EBIT) to remind ourselves as managers what elements require our continued attention to make our businesses survive. To distinguish between the accounting concept EBIT and my EBIT, let me refer to the latter as our Managerial EBIT or *M-EBIT.* Tongue in cheek, you could even refer to it as the *me bit,* the bit that we as managers have to attend to in order to be successful in our endeavors and earn our pay.

This turn of phrase *M-EBIT* can be broken down as follows:

- *M* stands for *managerial.*
- *E* stands for *environment.*
- *B* stands for *business.*
- *I* stands for *I,* or me, myself.
- *T* stands for *team.*

For those of you paying close attention, you may respond at once and say, "Aha, but there is no *I* in team and therefore *I* should not be associated with *team,* and certainly not be mentioned or put before *team.* Shame on you; if that doesn't smack of self-interest what does?"

Not considering the fact that EBTI doesn't quite have the same ring as EBIT, there are very sound reasons for putting the *I* before the *T.* Please have a little patience, and I will explain in some detail why in my M-EBIT, the *I* of you, the manager, should be there and should even be positioned before team. It all has to do with a continued emphasis on setting the example and improving the world by starting with oneself. As a second very important reason, one must not forget that there most definitely is a *me* in team. If you cannot find the motivation and satisfaction in leading, and often also in participating on a particular team, the chances are that you are not passionate enough about the common objective of that team. Then, as the somewhat candid saying goes, "shape up or ship out."

THE *E* IN M-EBIT

Our business operates in its own environment, but from time to time the macroenvironment impinges on this microenvironment. The macroenvironment consists of all the things that we, as individuals or as individual businesses, have little influence on, although all of us shape the macroenvironment. Typical examples on how the macroenvironment influences our own environment are the rules and regulations laid down by governments and other legislative bodies, the weather, infrastructure, currency fluctuations, major conflicts, and so on. Also more and more important are the often still-developing rules and regulations that govern what we as a society, including our businesses, are allowed to do in order to minimize the impact on the physical environment. Measuring one's "carbon footprint" is certainly becoming popular. To comply with all these rules and regulations and still remain competitive will surely be a challenge for a lot of businesses in the future. As a manager, it is important to be aware of the forces that shape the macroenvironment and their impact on our own microenvironment.[1] After all, no man is an island, but our main focus should be on our business's microenvironment.

Your Microenvironment and All Your Stakeholders

Under microenvironment we can group all the things that can directly influence our business, such as the stakeholders and our location. Stakeholders in our business are our customers, competitors, shareholders, financiers, suppliers, and employees. All these stakeholders determine our microenvironment and how successful we will be in that environment. Some of these stakeholders we can choose ourselves, but others are thrust upon us. Customers are the most critical of our stakeholders, and therefore we should spend a considerable amount of our time deciding who we, as a business, want our customers to be. The most difficult thing in business is to learn to say "no" when what is being asked is clearly beyond the scope of our business. If you go to the corner hardware store and ask for a loaf of bread, the proprietor will politely refer you, we can but hope, to the local baker. If you go to the baker and ask her for two ounces of thinly sliced ham, she will again, politely, we assume, refer you to the butcher.

In all these clear-cut examples, the mentioned businesses focus on their respective specialties. Sometimes the boundaries get blurred. For example, the bakery that starts selling ready-to-eat ham sandwiches, and the hardware store that operates a snack rack. Whether this is clever or not is not for me to decide. What is clear is that by moving away from one's basic specialty, a wholly unrelated set of additional challenges are added to the business. Not only does the baker need to make sure that her bread is well kept and fresh, but she also needs to make sure that the ham she procures is fresh, is stored separately from the bread, and does not spoil. After all, the customer who buys the ham sandwich will hold her responsible for the freshness, quality, and taste of that sandwich.

Your Customers Your Stakeholders

The importance of deciding who your customers are and therefore also when to say "no" politely is often the most difficult decision any growing business will have to make.[2] It also stands to reason that during a downturn any business will try to start stretching or even redefining the principle of who their real customers are. If this is done intentionally with the necessary service structure in place, there is nothing wrong with that.

Obviously this can be done from both ends, product and customer, by changing your product to suit a different group of customers, the lunch crowd for the baker example above, or by addressing a new group of customers and creating interest in your existing range of products. It certainly could be classified as *innovation,* as long as you realize that the business will again have to define who is this new group of customers, and how you can serve them best. Sound management must resist the internal and external pressures to force new business into "old holes." These holes already exist, and to force the existing structure to operate under new conditions is a sure road to chaos at best, or disaster at worst. You often have to jump out of existing structures to let new business in. But that is an internal or "black box" problem. The big C opportunity is to redefine your customer base to include the new opportunities. But do redefine it properly. Not making clear whom you want your customers to be, your big C, will lead to endless internal and external difficulties. *You can truly say that our customers are our business if you and your staff know who your customers are.*

Your Suppliers Your Stakeholders

Your suppliers are a very important part of your microenvironment. The notion that no suppliers = no customers = no products must start at making sure that you select your suppliers carefully. But also make sure that your business gets value for its money. The emphasis here is on value because it's value that must decide what the best supplier arrangements are for your business. Particularly in a downturn, the structured process of an inverse marketing campaign will help you find that value. It's based on the premise that you take purchasing out of its day-to-day operating environment and put it squarely at the very top of the organization during the campaign. A dollar saved in purchasing drops directly and without dilution to your bottom line. That's a reward well worth the management time, I would think.

Your Financiers Your Stakeholders

To manage your organization's relations with its financiers takes on a different meaning in a crisis. Bankers get even more nervous and want to reduce risk as much as possible. So feed your bankers more information than you normally would, in order to keep them informed of your current position. Surprise them by being proactive in this respect, and give them as much information about your position as possible. If you have untapped credit lines, draw them down in order to have access to the funds. In difficult times, cash is king, and the more flexibility you have, the better.

If you do have a real innovation to bring to market, don't only talk to your traditional bank(s), but seek other means of getting finance as well, such as venture capital. Venture capitalists are always on the lookout for real opportunities, and genuine innovation is certainly one of these. Conventional wisdom states that if you have such a daring venture, you should build it in tough times. Then you can launch it when the worst is over, and exit when boom returns. It's what I call the "fairy tale come true" scenario. Again, don't mix it with your existing business; remember what we said earlier under "Your Customers Your Stakeholders," and develop it as a separate venture with separate resources and its own organizational structure.

Stakeholders You Can't Choose

Just because in general you can't choose your shareholders and competitors, that doesn't mean that you don't have to manage them. Particularly in the case of shareholders, it is very important to give them the confidence that it is business as usual by feeding them regular updates. Realize that the moment you communicate with them, you communicate with the whole environment, micro- and macro-, so don't say anything that you haven't already told your staff, or that you don't want your competitors to know. In public companies, an inordinate amount of time is spent on shareholder relations, but even in a smaller and private setting you should not dismiss this as being over the top. If your shareholder is a single entrepreneur who is not active in the business, treat her like a shareholder. It wouldn't be the first time that an entrepreneur got cold feet and sold the business without consulting her senior management, including the general manager. Thus keep close to your single "shareholder," and communicate.

Competition is difficult to manage, and perhaps one should not even attempt to do so. In every downturn there will be efforts by competitors, sometimes in the guise of industry federations, to fix prices. Nobody will call it that. After all, that is illegal, but it happens, and the temptation is always there. There are plenty of industry cartels. Some of them, such as OPEC, have to be tolerated. Some others are exposed from time to time by belated government action. It is never in the interest of customers to fix prices. Customers are entitled to value for money, too, and they have the right to decide for themselves what value means to them. Just watch competitors closely, but don't get carried away. *One of the well-known commandments for losing in business is this: Concentrate on the competition rather than on the customer.* Any strategy based on what the competition does is by definition reactive. Reactive strategies should not always be shunned, but they should never take precedence over a proactive approach. A proactive approach tends to focus on the customer, not on the competition or even on the product.

Taking over a competitor or a business that will add value to your own should be approached with extreme caution. The failure rate of mergers is well above 75%, and with odds like that, you and your team need to be really determined and have the resources to make it work over time.

THE *B* IN M-EBIT

The second letter of my anagram refers to our own business. And because our own business revolves around its well-defined customers, we can safely say that customers are the reward challenge. The ultimate reward of any business is satisfied customers. They always are and always will be, regardless of the economic climate. Lose your customers, and all your other challenges will disappear like snow before the sun. They don't matter anymore, and they will melt and even evaporate without a trace of their past perceived importance because your organization will cease to exist. *No customers = No Business.* As long as you have customers, you are doing something right, so find out what it is that you do well and make it even better.

Customers are really quite undemanding. Yes, they really are! As long as they get what you promised them, they won't unduly "bother" you. You can get on with all those lovely problems that need to be solved in the black box. Don't give them what you promised, and you'd better correct it smartly and apologize profusely. Then they might "bother" you again for a repeat order. So "keep 'em happy and coming" is the motto. Never be too busy to deal with a customer, even if that is not your main function! If the organization can change its mentality from "being bothered" by customers to "looking forward to interruption" by customers, you have achieved a true turnaround. It is not as easy as it sounds. The sting lies in the detail, but because not many organizations truly practice what they preach with regard to customer service there is real opportunity to outdo your competitors in a downturn.

The Differentiation and Innovation Challenge

Look for every opportunity to make your products or services just that little bit different from those of your competitors. Even changes that seemingly have nothing to do with the product itself can make a difference. This continuous quest for differentiation might even lead to a breakthrough and a genuine innovation. Keep challenging your team and evaluate all serious suggestions. Watch your market and try and distinguish new and upcoming trends. See how you can apply them and profit without making large commitments that you probably cannot afford at the present. Practice all those cheap marketing tools that we discussed at length, and do not hide behind slogans and expensive marketing campaign to show the flag. Rather, be right on the ball and actually run with it continually. Actions speak much louder than words, particularly when customers become more discerning and are bombarded with continuous efforts to part them from their hard-earned cash.

The "Live Within Your Means" Challenge

A downturn is certainly an appropriate time to learn to live within your means as an organization and sometimes even as an individual. We were all caught up in easy credit and our organizations were no different. A close examination of all the required costs to keep operating effectively, albeit at a reduced level, is probably long overdue. An unfortunate consequence of living within our corporate means often involves staff redundancies. When the chips are really down, and voluntary cuts in salaries, reduced working hours, and three-day weeks are no longer enough, redundancies will have to be faced. If this has to be, you can at least make sure it happens in a humane fashion. Treat every victim as you would like to be treated. It's the least you can do for those who used to be part of the team, too.

The RCF Challenge

The close monitoring and detailed management of the real cash flow (RCF) is one of the main technical ingredients for survival. Never mind about all the accounting concepts, such as profit or loss or application of funds, EBIT, and others. Just concentrate on the real cash flow. If you can give the cash flow a boost by means of one-time actions, old stock, and so forth, do it now! Don't wait for the price of scrap metal to go up, or the demand for an old stock item to increase; you need the cash now! Solve those long-running customer disputes, and settle! Fifty percent of a large outstanding amount is more useful than a pending court action that you are convinced you will win (but the other party begs to differ). Narrow the gap between cash out and cash in as best you can. The principles are pretty straightforward, but the snake in the grass is the detail, as always. Make sure that it is everybody's business, and follow up continually on who does what when it comes to debtors and creditors. A real team effort involving management, an inverse marketing campaign, sales personnel, accounts, and any other relevant department will bear fruit—or cash, to be precise.

THE *I* IN M-EBIT

There are very convenient, but also very sound, reasons why the *I* comes before the *T* of team in M-EBIT. First of all, every team needs an effective leader, and as a manager you must be that team leader. Don't beat about the bush in times of real crises: You can't always seek and achieve consensus, but decide first and explain afterwards. That is also part of being a team leader.

It has everything to do with starting a change from individual focus to team focus with yourself. My most potent premise of effective management is based on leading by example. Maybe it is not very sophisticated; it certainly doesn't sound involved, it does not require years of study—but it requires loads of practice. It is extremely difficult to apply continually and consistently. The sting as always is in the detail. Nevertheless, if you practice setting the example, particularly in difficult times, you will find that leading your management and the overall team will be a lot easier. Unfortunately the "lead by example" principle has been badly mauled by the "me first" attitude of a very long boom period. So to get back to a less selfish basis is not going to be easy. However, I for one am absolutely convinced that if we, as managers, can get the "I and me" back to the "I set the example for the team," we will conquer any downturn and have an excellent chance of coming out so much stronger than we went in.

The Personal Change Challenge

Coping with a downturn also revolves around dealing with change. For the past twenty years or so, the only hymn book available was the "hit song book of growth" and how to achieve it. Consequently a whole generation of managers has grown up with only those hymns uppermost on their minds. Couple to this the attention given to science and systems in management, and you have a potentially fragile and misleading mix to address "life" people issues. And change is all about people. Change is not endlessly quibbling and theorizing about the way the organization should be but rather mobilizing action among employees. Also, successful change must always start with yourself. In change management jargon, "management must align its own behavior with the objective." As you know by now, I much prefer "lead by example." Most formal change programs fail because top management does not feel the need "to align its behavior with the objective," and leading by example sounds far too committed and permanent. It's much easier to hide behind all the jargon and hold on to your own ways and privileges while the organization suffers from your "decisive" actions. But if you do start to lead by example, you will reach a much better platform for the changes you have to introduce in order to survive. "Change the world, and start with yourself" is a pretty sound principle, not only for environmentalists, but also for managers.

The Personal "It's All in the Detail" Challenge

Business is all about the detail. It's not about coming up with the big ideas and then assuming that everybody else will attend to the detail. It's about assuming that no one will do the detail, and that you have to make sure that people attend to it. Follow up continually and constructively.

Particularly in a downturn when strategy perhaps needs to be reviewed, targets are wishful thinking, and budgets have become superfluous it's absolutely critical not to spend too much time on all that stuff, during working hours anyway. Just attend to the detail day in and day out. Get the detail right, and you will have an excellent chance to hold on to your existing customers and perhaps even acquire some new ones.

The Personal Listening and Communication Challenge

Now is the time to really sharpen your listening and observational skills. By listening actively to your customers, to your staff, and to the other noises in your environment, you might pick up hints for product differentiation ideas and other improvements. Start practicing the skills of listening at every opportunity you have. Set yourself the goal of reversing your talk-listen ratio, and actively work on it. It is an acquired skill that all of us can master.

Communication is a vital element in difficult times. Use it to your best advantage and to strengthen the team feeling and the customer bond. Be consistent in communications, and remember, don't make promises you can't keep. If you don't know, say you don't know. In a downturn the macroenvironment changes continually, and uncertainties are the order of the day. Don't make out that you have the answer. You are not a politician who lives on public appearances, nor are you a reporter who has to come up with another slant to sell copy.

The Personal "Be Humble" Challenge

There are three minimal phrases that should become part of your vocabulary as soon as possible. They are, *I don't know, I need help* and *I was wrong*. It is amazing how difficult it is for boom time managers to use and genuinely mean these simple confessions. Often more time is spent on defending the indefensible than on simply saying that you were wrong. It is as well to remember that a lasting impression will be created, not by the mistake itself, but rather by the manner in which the mistake was handled. A much better approach is to get excited about your mistakes and realize that you have learned something and cannot wait to try again. That is really turning a negative into a positive.

The "ask for help" thought is really showing that you are accepting the fact that you don't know everything, are very willing to learn, desire to expand your own knowledge, and are prepared to work with others. Let us not forget that organizations are built around helping each other and using the skills of all members of the team. It is all part of getting out of the me first mentality and the personal credit-seeking mode and putting more emphasis on the team and the achievements of the team. The beauty is that in such a scenario you will also get the credit, but in a different, much more rewarding, and constructive way.

"I don't know" is a very powerful phrase that is not used often enough. It is quite fascinating to see people squirm, argue, and bluff their way out of a "don't know" situation. As an interim general manager, I have frequently had to use this admission of not knowing something in new and unfamiliar circumstances. There is nothing wrong with not knowing something, as long as you are prepared to find out. So it makes sense that the expression, "I don't know, but I'll find out," is much more powerful than some misguided effort to cover up.

Even if you do know, or think you know, it might be advantageous to say something like, "I don't know, but it seems to me . . ." You often find out a lot more this way, particularly in customer contact situations. Not admitting what you don't know might make some people wonder about what you actually do know. So here again it's not a weakness but a strength to admit that you don't really know.

Naturally you must strike a balance in using the above expressions. If you go around all day long proclaiming that you don't know, you need help, and you were wrong, your team members or your boss might just start to think that you have a self-punishing streak, are going around like a bat in daylight, or have a learning disability. But most of us, managers I mean, will find it difficult enough to admit to these three notions, so when the occasion strikes, be honest with yourself, and use it when you truly mean it. Honesty beyond everything and being interested in other people's opinions are key to using the powerful notions of *I don't know, I need help,* and *I was wrong.* Don't abuse, but use!

THE *T* IN M-EBIT

Team has been the recurring malpractice suit of the latest boom period. Individualism and self-gratification took over. The latest boom period was characterized by huge, unbelievable differences in reward between the few at the top and the rest of us. In quite a few large organizations, the CEO now earns 500 times as much as the average worker in his company. How can one talk about being on the same team when you are not even on the same planet—never mind the same league? About 225 years ago, the French Revolution was fought, and some form of equality was painfully regained because the difference between the haves and the have-nots had reached ludicrous proportions. Will history repeat itself in our lifetime in a modern variation of this historic event?

To recover the essence of team play with effective contributions from all employees won't be easy, but will depend very much on the example that we set as managers. Lead by example again and again. Don't expect quick results, but you will see steady progress if all the participants start understanding that it's the new game in town, and they must take it seriously. Make it a team sport, and you will get team players. If you don't, all the ambitious star seekers, including you, will eventually realize that you might be brilliant individually, but as a team you stink. Good teams do have star players, but in the right setting even they will realize that they can be stars only because of the efforts of the whole team (and nothing but the team).

Your Stakeholders Your Team

In all the years I have practiced as a general manager, three things have really stood out in all the various countries, industries, and companies that I have had the pleasure to be closely involved with:

1. How much other employees contributed, and how much they enjoyed being made to feel part of it.
2. How important it is for employees to enjoy their jobs and give 110%.
3. The importance of the detail.

Sometimes as victims of our ambition and our misplaced feeling of self-worth, we tend to forget those very basic facts. Those facts were true 25 years ago before we even dreamed of being considered as knowledge workers, and they are still true today, with the latest crop of employees, the Net Geners, hitting the labor market. Personal star ambitions and star indulgence have been pretty disturbing factors in our society, and renewed recognition of team play and team effort are long overdue. Although it is true that team leadership is critical, the team itself needs to acknowledge and respect that fact in order to perform at its best. Respect has to be earned and can never be demanded. The well-known expression, "If you can't get respect, you settle for fear," is a poor substitute for a lack of true management skills. But if one acknowledges that most employees want to enjoy their jobs, and, what is more, like to enjoy the feeling of being part of a team, then the battle has an excellent chance of being won. These realities are a pretty good basis for tackling the difficult conditions of a downturn.

THE ALTOGETHER NOW M-EBIT

The ultimate challenge is to make it all happen like a well-rehearsed symphony performed by a well-directed, trained, committed, and evenly balanced orchestra. Of course the customer must always come first, but all the other bits and pieces in the black box need to happen too. So let all employees sing in unison from the current "challenging times" hymn sheet; that is your main task as a manager. Define and maintain the vision, and build a great team. Don't be the star performer nor the "hide behind my incompetent subordinates" coward, but the "it is my responsibility" team leader who pays great attention to the detail, follows up, corrects, teaches, supports, encourages, and expects 110% because he himself gives 125%!

The "Correct and Refine" Challenge

Then, when it is all starting to happen, and occasionally things go wrong, it is time for the nonstop process of correcting and refining. Correcting is necessary to make sure that the course is kept and that little bad habits do not grow into major flaws. It is oh-so-easy to make exceptions and think, "oh, well; I'll attend to that tomorrow." Just attend to it now because tomorrow there will be other bits of detail that need attending to. We need refining because sometimes adjustments are necessary to make what we do even more effective or to cater to changing circumstance or shifts in customer demands. An organization should be a "living organism" that adjusts itself to new challenges presented by its customers, or that appeals to a different group of customers.

Once the major adjustments are made to cope with a serious downturn, you might have to make many adjustments to stay in the game. Retain the vision and continually reinforce what it is that needs to be achieved. Modern employees will certainly be keen to contribute their own efforts if they are left to their own resources. "Not tramlines, but guidelines," should be the motto. After all, it's not how it is done but that it is done and done in such a way that the end result is achieved. Then when economic times return for the better, you and your team will be ready to reap what was sown during the difficult times. It's a team challenge that will be extremely satisfying for all the stakeholders.

THE VERY LAST CHALLENGE

Let me conclude with the crucial test for you, the reader, who took this journey from reality checks and relearning to appropriate opportunities via what can be controlled and the focus on the basics to summarize it all with M-EBIT. If you conclude that you were already doing most of these things, then you are still in denial. Are you sure you haven't glossed over those sections in which your own business practices could stand the most improvement? You haven't accepted yet that we were not really that good, and that economic boom circumstances were very much responsible for past achievements. Complacency, smugness, and egotism are the most menacing forces in business; taken together, they are powerful enough to prevent real positive change. You are well advised to take heed of the business paradox, *the better you think you are doing, the greater should be your cause for concern.* Put differently, the more self-satisfied you are with your past accomplishments, your past decisions, and your reputation, the less you should be.

Stripped of all its jargon, knowledge, skills, and systems, management is essentially an "it's all in the mind" game. Of course the knowledge and skills are very important, but they are not the determining factors of what makes a truly effective manager. The real edge of that is in the mind. That sense of dissatisfaction with your own achievements and the promise to yourself that you will definitely do better "next time." So let's get on with it now; today is important; there is no time to waste.

Let's even do better THIS TIME!
M-EBIT, or the ME BIT, once more:

- *M* is for Management.
- *E* is for your Environment.
- *B* is for your Business.
- *I* is for you, the "I Lead by Example" You.
- *T* is for your team.

And then,
The DETAIL, always the DETAIL!

A Fairy Tale Revisited: Snow White and the Seven Dwarfs, or, the Result of an Ultimate Service Economy[1]

Once there were seven dwarfs who lived just behind the rugged range of the seven mountains. Day in and day out they slaved in their underground mine in one of the seven mountains and dug for gold nuggets. Which one of the mountains had and probably still has gold nuggets hidden in its many crevices is known only to the local dwarfs! Each one of the dwarfs was honest and hardworking, and they all respected one another. When one of them got tired, he rested and none of the others minded. When one of them needed something, the others gave readily and with great pleasure. In the evening when the day's work was done, they ate their bread together and went to bed. On the seventh day they did not work, but took a well-deserved rest.

SEVEN MINUS ONE

One day one of the dwarfs suggested that they didn't actually know how much their efforts were really worth. He started to count the nuggets that were brought to the surface. And while he was busy counting, the other ones did his share of the work. Soon enough he took this "nugget counting" so seriously that he started to count full-time, and hence had to put down his shovel forever. That's when his six friends started to grumble and complain. They looked at the activities of the seventh dwarf with some suspicion and started to query his counting activities. The nugget-counting dwarf was taken aback and defended these activities; the counting was vital, he said, so they would know what had actually been accomplished. The others did not really grasp this concept, but they gave him the benefit of the doubt. And although he could no longer relate his newly selected career to the day-to-day work of the other dwarfs, they all still sat at the same table. The other dwarfs saw the stacks of paper and figures created by the "nugget counter," but they shook their heads because they did not really understand what he was doing.

SEVEN MINUS TWO

It didn't take long before the "accountant"—that's what he had started to call himself—came with his next proposal. He suggested that each dwarf account for his own production of nuggets and sign for it on what he called a "work sheet." The six dwarfs, who were, by the way, still slaving day in and day out, were furious about this request and started to object forcefully, in a dwarf sense of course. This worried the accountant sufficiently for him to persuade one of the other dwarfs to take on the responsibility of leading the remaining five workers. The newly appointed leader called himself "manager" and naturally had to lay down his shovel as well. So now, only five of the dwarfs still worked in the mine. Of course, they were still expected to produce what seven of them had a while back.

The motivation of the five working dwarfs got worse by the day, but what could they actually do about it? When the manager heard their complaints, he thought long and hard and sold them the concept of "specialization" as a means of increasing overall production. Thus each one of the remaining five workers would complete a specific task according to his individual talents. Some dug using the picks, some shoveled the dirt, and one operated the wheelbarrow.

Unfortunately, this latest fad did nothing to lighten the load of the five workers; production did not increase, and, what's more, when one of them was sick, output came to a grinding halt. Reassigning the duties of a sick dwarf among his colleagues became a nightmare. As specialists they were no longer the same, and they even resented taking on additional duties.

SEVEN MINUS THREE

The newly appointed manager felt that his former colleagues and friends did not really appreciate the importance of his many arduous tasks. Somehow or other his popularity was not what he thought it should have been, given the "enormous" responsibilities that he shouldered. Thus, in order to improve communications with the workforce, he decided to appoint one of them as supervisor. The supervisor was going to be the link between the manager and the "workforce." Naturally, the supervisor put down his tools and started waving his arms about in an effort to drive the remaining four dwarfs on to greater efforts. Unfortunately the mood among the four dwarfs did not improve at all, nor did their output. More and more, the supervisor was seen in the office with the manager in what they called "meetings." Even at night "management," that is, the accountant, the manager, and the supervisor, spent many hours drinking coffee in The White as Snow local pub, run by Snow White, where they sat hunched together in a corner, discussing the day's nugget production and the many reports produced by the accountant. The four "employees"—that's what management had started to call the remaining workers—watched TV and drank their well-earned beers at the bar after a hard day's work.

To try to improve morale, the manager decided to organize an outing for the employees to a nearby amusement park. To make sure that gold production was not affected, the tour took place on the weekend. Also, to make sure that the outing could be classed as a business expense, the manager gave a long lecture, in which he used the jargon that he had acquired at a thirteen-day, part-time executive development program, EDP for those of you in the know, from a renowned business school.

One day it came to open conflict. The workers threw their little tools down, stamped their little feet, and made little fists. The manager got a real fright and promised to recruit some new workers who would help the four dwarfs achieve the production targets that the accountant had assured him were necessary to retain profitability. Thus, five new dwarfs were recruited from another community.

SEVEN MINUS FOUR PLUS FIVE

In order to control the foreign dwarfs, the manager decided to appoint one of the local dwarfs as supervisor for the foreign team. The chosen dwarf duly laid down his shovel. The accountant came up with a brilliant scheme to measure the output of each team individually and introduce some internal competition by setting challenging targets. Unfortunately the two teams, the foreign labor team of five, and in particular the remaining three dwarfs who formed the local team, did not get into the spirit of things. The two teams looked at each other with distrust, complained, and seldom cooperated in their daily work routine.

The manager was getting quite frustrated by this eternal bickering and decided that what was needed was a human resources advisor. One of the three local dwarfs was fittingly appointed, laid down his shovel, moved to the office next to the manager, and was never seen underground again.

SEVEN MINUS FIVE PLUS FIVE MINUS FIVE

The two remaining working dwarfs appeared to be even more de-motivated than before and found continuous fault with management and the foreign team. In the meanwhile, the accountant had computed that the foreign workers generated more expenses than benefits, and the human resources advisor intimated that indirectly this fact, coupled with the "unhealthy level of competition," was in all probability the cause of the overall poor performance. The manager had no choice but to lay off all foreign workers and rely solely on the local team. The dwarf who had been appointed to supervise the guest workers could not possibly be asked to revert back to employee status. Opportunely a vacancy for an assistant accountant had arisen due to the inordinate amount of analyses asked for by management and carried out by the accountant. The burden and workload of generating these requests, coupled with his own work to try to pinpoint the cause for the fall in production was getting to be too much for him, and help was needed badly!

Unfortunately all the calculations, analyses, and charts in the world failed to point to a single, particular problem. Thus the manager decided to seek advice from a well-known and greatly esteemed management consultant. This consultant spent quite some time discussing the problems with management before paying a visit to the underground and real "nugget face." He interviewed both the remaining workers, strolled aimlessly but arrogantly through the mine, and observed the process of digging for nuggets for a few minutes. In his comprehensive and detailed report, he described the nugget extraction process in a series of multicolored foldout diagrams supported by many pages of elaborate text, suitably interspaced with complex graphics and tables that completely and utterly baffled the manager. Being a "graduate" of a renowned business school's EDP program, he obviously couldn't admit to this lack of understanding! On the last page of this well-presented and extensive report, the consultant concluded that the most likely grounds for the bad performance could more than likely be found in some of the work practices. He had observed that the last two dwarfs working in the mine were not using their picks and shovels correctly. His recommendation was a further study, by him, naturally, with an emphasis on what he called, "time and motion," to determine the root cause of this work deficiency. Then he presented his invoice, was paid a bucketful of nuggets, and disappeared as fast as he had arrived.

SEVEN MINUS SIX PLUS NOTHING

In the meantime, the two dwarfs who were by now solely responsible for the total nugget output decided to form a labor union to protect their jobs and to shield themselves from management interference in their accepted and well-established work practices. One of them was elected union representative. He duly laid down his tools, and so only one worker remained. Naturally, management now had to agree to his working conditions through the union representative, and after many lengthy and intricate negotiations, a deal appeared to be in the making. Unfortunately, the last working dwarf appeared uninterested and unmotivated. To cope with his lonely time at the nugget face, he had accepted a part-time job as a waiter at the White as Snow Inn during the evening hours. Being left to his own resources during the long underground day, he did take the odd catnap to keep his strength up and to be prepared for his second job.

Not long afterward the accountant and his assistant worked out that the mine was no longer viable. The accountant, the manager, the assistant accountant, the supervisor, and the human resources advisor allocated themselves substantial severance payments and left in a hurry to avoid charges of fraud.

COULD IT HAPPEN?

So now you know the real story of Snow White and the Seven Dwarfs. It's such a shocking tale of "what can happen if . . . ," that someone just had to distort it into a sweet fairy tale that would appeal to children and their parents alike. Hence the star role played by Snow White. The bit about the apple and the prince was somewhat far-fetched, but it was strangely satisfying. After all, the truth is much, much more alarming.

And what happened to the last remaining working dwarf? No one really knows, but if you come across a tiny disgruntled dwarf, who has no time for all that fancy management stuff, hates nugget counters, finds his supervisor objectionable, loathes the human resources advisor, has left the union, and just gets on with his job, be considerate. He fulfills a key function, and he knows it!

SOME BACKGROUND TO TERMS SUCH AS KNOWLEDGE ECONOMY AND KNOWLEDGE WORKERS

KNOWLEDGE AND A KNOWLEDGE ECONOMY

Some of the confusion and awkwardness about knowledge and knowledge economy has probably arisen because of the use of the word *knowledge* itself. After all, less-developed, and even what we now consider primitive, societies relied on some sort of knowledge. The basic machines of classical antiquity are living proof of this.[1]

Not disputed is that technology, or *prescriptive knowledge* in the jargon, was the basis of the industrial revolution that probably started in the late 1700s. Since then the historical model of advances in science and of propositional knowledge leading to technological progress or prescriptive knowledge has been superseded by the interaction between the two. Technology affected science as much as the other way round. The economic history of the twentieth century shows that many modern technological advances were in place before the First World War (1914–1918). They just needed continued development and improvement to make their mark on daily life.[2] So to talk about knowledge as a recently invented phenomenon is in truth quite misleading, as is the common popular notion that we are witnessing a revolution wherein all people "work with their brains instead of their hands." These are lovely and catchy simplifications, but they are totally void of reality and even demeaning to the millions of qualified technicians who work with their hands *and* their brains.

Nevertheless, the overall picture is this: knowledge, from its relatively modest beginnings, is now one of the major driving forces that propel economies to ever-higher levels. In *Working for the Future: Technology and Employment in the Global Knowledge Economy*, Sheehan and Tegart[3] reported that

> The knowledge economy is emerging from two defining forces: the rise in *knowledge intensity* of economic activities, and the increasing *globalization* of economic affairs.

The rise in knowledge intensity is being driven by the combined forces of the information technology revolution and the increasing pace of technological change. Globalization is being driven by national and international deregulation, and by the IT-related communications revolution. However, it is important to note that the term "knowledge economy" refers to the overall economic structure that is emerging, not to any one, or [a] combination of these phenomena.

Thus it is not knowledge on its own that is leading us into a new era of development. Rather it is the increasing use of global knowledge and our ability to distribute this knowledge effectively, exemplified by the Internet, which is changing the business environment dramatically. Some unique characteristics of knowledge are these:

(a) Once knowledge is known, it is never forgotten. It can be duplicated ad nauseam, often with minimal costs.[4]
(b) Ideas and innovations have extensive externalities. Once development has taken place, their use requires only some rudimentary knowledge. For example, the average consumer needs no knowledge about wave propagation theory, the principles of electronics, plasma screen technology, battery manufacture, and so forth, to use a cell phone.
(c) Knowledge for its own sake is declining relative to useful knowledge, that is, "to know" is nice to know, but "to know how to use" is vital. That is also one of the reasons why education has become a lifelong experience.

The above attributes have assisted in propelling the intensity of knowledge to its present significance, thus making it the main driving force of the modern economy.

Globalization is the second major contributing force that is emerging as a real influencing factor in the post-industrial era. Increasingly, goods and services are no longer bound by national boundaries or transportation costs. The possible instant worldwide recognition of products, thanks to the Internet, has led to a global market place in which consumers, but also companies, use their newfound power to look for value and satisfaction.

WHAT THEN IS A KNOWLEDGE WORKER?

Having established that knowledge has been around for some time and is increasingly part of our society, what then is meant by a knowledge worker? In an article for the *Economist*, Peter Drucker expressed his opinion as follows:

At present, this term [knowledge worker] is widely used to describe people with considerable theoretical knowledge and learning: doctors, lawyers, teachers, accountants, chemical engineers. But the most striking growth will be in "knowledge technologists": computer technicians, software designers, analysts in clinical labs, manufacturing technologists, paralegals. These people are as much manual workers as they are knowledge workers; in fact, they usually spend far more time working with their hands than with their brains. But their manual work is based on a substantial amount of theoretical knowledge, which can be acquired only through formal education, not through an apprenticeship.[5]

If one considers that the modern-day variety of the established apprenticeship system in many countries often entails a substantial element of classroom instruction, the divide between apprenticeship and formal education becomes somewhat blurred. Thus, even employees in the so-called trades can lay claim to being "knowledge workers." In an earlier article, Drucker had this to say on the subject:

In the amount and kind of formal knowledge required, knowledge work will differ tremendously. Some will have fairly low requirements; some will require the kind of knowledge the neurosurgeon has to possess. Even if the knowledge itself is quite primitive, it is knowledge that only formal education can provide. Filing is hardly advanced knowledge work. However, it is based on the knowledge of the alphabet, or in Japan on a knowledge of Chinese ideographs, which can be acquired only in and through systematic learning, that is, in and through formal schooling.[6]

Thus to my mind the group of so-called knowledge workers is ever increasing, and the difference between knowledge worker and nonknowledge worker is becoming more and more ambiguous. Perhaps we should approach the matter differently by asking ourselves the question, what is nonknowledge work? Is it perhaps manual work? Not according to Drucker, who explains that knowledge work will require high manual skills and substantial work with one's hands, and gives as an extreme example the work of the neurosurgeon. So if it's not manual labor, what then is nonknowledge work? Is an assembly worker who repeats the same manual motions time and time again a nonknowledge worker? What about the waiter or waitress who takes your order for lunch, using one of those online dedicated handheld terminals? Is it the insurance clerk, who feeds the system with your personal and policy details? The office cleaner, or, if you like the modern version, the sanitation engineer? The shop assistant who tries to help you decide on a purchase? The supermarket person who restocks the shelves? All of these workers have acquired skills, manual and nonmanual, that require formal basic skills and specific skills that nowadays require frequent updates.[7]

Fortunately, some pragmatism about the whole subject of knowledge and knowledge workers was introduced by Robert Reich and Kit Sims Taylor.[8] The latter wrote,

> With this new era [the era of the knowledge worker] has come such a proliferation of terms that we hardly know what to call ourselves or our new world. Peter Drucker coined the term *knowledge worker* in 1959, but left the definition rather fuzzy. In 1991 Robert Reich put us into the narrower—but more carefully defined—category of *symbolic analyst*. With our fingers on our mice and our minds in cyberspace, do we toil in Drucker's *knowledge society,* Manual Castells's *network society* or *Wired's new economy?* It matters little what we decide to call ourselves—we are the masters of the information technology revolution and the creators of the information that seems to be the driving force behind a long boom. Secure in an economy which finds ever-new uses for our mental creations, we fail to ask the obvious question: *What comes after knowledge work.*[9]

Maybe, after all, a clear distinction between knowledge worker and non-knowledge worker is not really that critical in the context of describing modern-day (2009) work requirements and its effect on management practices. Perhaps it is much more useful to note that modern business practice has a continuous requirement for employees who know how to learn in a variety of settings, formal and informal, well past the stage of initial schooling.

KNOWLEDGE WORKER PERFORMANCE

If we are still unclear about what really constitutes the group of knowledge workers, it becomes pretty difficult to describe what their performance should be. The management literature on knowledge-worker performance totally ignores the vast army of knowledge workers who are subject to pretty acceptable work practices and performance criteria, and it appears to concentrate instead on that small band of elusive, hard-to-pin-down specialists in the IT arena. The latter relatively small group is indeed difficult to control in the traditional sense. Time management means nothing to them, but when they are "in the groove," they will work all hours of the day and night. So allow flextime, and be plenty understanding of their positive attributes, but often negative behavior. They tend to overpromise and underdeliver, and they need a "father" management figure to oversee their output and performance.[10] The debate is almost a repeat of the academic discussions of days past on how to control output in research laboratories or research establishments, and the almost forgotten topic of "human resources accounting.[11] Davenport, Thomas, and Cantrell reported on a year-long study to investigate the mysteries of what they termed knowledge workers and concluded that organizations can't begin to increase their understanding of what makes knowledge workers effective until they recognize the importance of such workers as a whole and how to differentiate among them as individuals.[12] In another article Tom Davenport said,

> When it comes to knowledge workers, we pretty much hire smart people and leave them alone. No quality measurements, no Six Sigma, no reengineering. We haven't formally examined the flow of work, we have no benchmarks, and there is no accountability for the cost and time these activities consume. As a result, we have little sense of whether they could do better.[13]

Unfortunately, for the majority of knowledge workers the above deliberations on the performance of their efforts is not really applicable. To my mind the term "knowledge worker" is far too vague and ill defined to address specific items such as performance and management to this group as a whole. It's like addressing industrial workers as a group without taking cognizance of the various specializations within the main category. It has always been difficult to determine "performance criteria" for certain types of workers. For example, take the multifunctional teams involved in the design and testing of a new car model. Although the flow of actual design work is not as neatly directed as the actual production side that follows, deadlines are, more often than not, met. Output is adjusted by the individual members of the team in "burning the midnight oil" sessions if required. Or take the paramedic, who is attending to a roadside victim. We can't apply the same criteria to her than we can to a programmer who needs to codify part of a well-thought-out routine, or an engineer who is designing a detail for an aircraft door to a strict deadline to fit in with other development work. No employee should be above output requirements unless she is a proven genius who provides real leaps for an organization's processes or products at regular intervals.

EDUCATION AND CONTINUOUS LEARNING

There is definitely an ever-increasing demand for educated workers in our modern Western society. Education can no longer be viewed as a one-time exercise administered early in life. More and more education must be viewed as a continuous learning experience throughout one's lifetime that can take place in formal or informal settings. Therefore, the ability and willingness to learn will be one of the greatest assets that an employee brings to an organization. The obvious danger of this is that immediately usable practical knowledge will be overvalued, and the importance of fundamental and general knowledge will be underrated. Another consequence of the voracious demand for specific education is the decline in what used to be referred to as general knowledge. Until quite recently a person was considered to be educated if he or she possessed a common base of formal general knowledge that was usually obtained by the study of liberal arts. In fact, liberal arts colleges prepared students for nothing practical, and they were, rightly or wrongly, proud of that fact. The demise of liberal arts is not altogether surprising. There was always a certain amount of skepticism by staff and students who followed more directional courses, such as, accountancy or engineering. But in these subjects specialization is more and more the order of the day because of the depth of knowledge required for what were in the past considered to be small subsets of the main area. Is earlier and earlier specialization the answer?

Thus in summary there are three distinct trends that are recognized as critical requirements for a modern society, namely,

(a) Formal education is often a first necessity.
(b) Specific education geared to usable practical knowledge is becoming paramount.
(c) Learning is a continuous process, well beyond the formal schooling years.

To throw a monkey wrench into this particular work, Paul Krugman in his "2096 article for the New York Times looking back" had this to say on the devaluation of higher education,

> In the 1990s everyone believed that education was the key to economic success, for both individuals and nations. A college degree, maybe even a postgraduate degree, was essential for anyone who wanted a good job as one of those "symbolic analysts." But computers are very good at analyzing symbols; it's the messiness of the real world they have trouble with. Furthermore symbols can be quite easily transmitted to Asmara or La Paz and analyzed there for a fraction of the cost of doing it in Boston.[1]

Maybe that was written somewhat "tongue in cheek" in 1996, but it should serve as a fair warning that the question posed by Kit Sims Taylor, "What comes after knowledge work?" might become pressing sooner rather than later, with the relentless spread of public domain knowledge via the Internet and the ease with which services can be transplanted to lower-wage environments.[2] Therefore, is sending everyone to a college or university the answer? Is formal classroom education in itself the answer? And if it is, what form should it take? What should be taught, and how? One thing is for certain: the mismatch between formal education and industry requirements has never been greater for the majority of the population. Just sending people to colleges and universities so that governments can proudly proclaim that it is their target that everyone is entitled to a university education might not be the answer. What is the point in spending four years at a college or university, and then spending the rest of one's life doing routine work, personal networking, promoting and socializing, and being engaged in creating knowledge that already exists elsewhere, but that is easier to reinvent than to find?

Perhaps the apprentice system, geared toward some formal but also practical know-how deserves to be reexamined.

GLOBALIZATION
VERSUS LOCALIZATION

Globalization is the second major contributing force that is emerging as a real influencing factor in the postindustrial era.[1] Increasingly, goods and services are no longer bound by national boundaries or transportation costs. The possible instant worldwide recognition of products, thanks to the Internet, has led to a global marketplace in which consumers use their newfound power to look for value and satisfaction. There are still quite a few limiting factors, such as trade barriers thrown up by countries, cartels, sole distributorships, and so forth, but the persistent trend in the Western World is to let "the invisible hand," as Adam Smith called it in 1776, shape events.[2]

Some of the major consequences of globalization for the business environment appear to have been the following:

- Competition takes place in the world market, even for niche products.
- Almost unrestricted movement of capital resources is now a reality.
- Protecting domestic markets is increasingly difficult.
- Production can be, and often is, rationalized on a global scale.
- International flows of goods are interdependent and interlinked.
- Specialization has resulted in increasingly complex production.
- Time is becoming really important for competitiveness.

Although the business environment has shown an increasing trend to globalize products and services, communities have shown an increasing desire to differentiate themselves on the basis of language or dialect, custom and/or culture, and sometimes even only location. These two opposing forces, the global marketplace versus local consumers, have been recognized for some time, but the consequences for the practice of management are becoming more and more profound. An article in the *Economist* on the increasing importance of the Welsh language in Wales noted the increase in the use of the Welsh language, particularly among the younger generation.[3] Given the nearness to England, the survival of Welsh is certainly remarkable, but not unique.[4] The Welsh language society, a pressure group, is continually trying to incorporate Welsh demands into law, such as the requirement to address customers in their preferred language. Welsh-speaking citizens are less likely to be unemployed and purportedly earn more than their monoglot English-speaking compatriots.

It's a fascinating example from within the United Kingdom. Mainland Europe offers a multitude of comparable scenarios across borders, but also frequently within sovereign states.[5] Similar conditions exist in the Americas, Asia, Africa, and the Middle East. On the one hand one expects management to think globally, but on the other hand one almost demands it to act locally. Even very large multinationals with plenty of international experience have been stumped by this phenomenon (witness the many cross-border mergers and acquisitions that have turned sour on the shareholders, in no mean part due to different cultures, norms, and values). In an era where less and less time is devoted to what in the English-speaking world is called "liberal arts," more and more managers have no reference framework at all to deal with different societies and cultures. For example, even if a foreign language is learned, it takes many years of practice and local interaction to communicate effectively and to become sensitized to the cultural differences.

SIX ADDITIONAL SEGMENTS THAT CAN OVERLAY AN EXISTING CUSTOMER MIX

Marketing experts have not been stupefied by the latest downturn. Instead they have tried to identify new spending-type groupings or segments to overlay existing consumer segments based on traditional parameters, such as lifestyle, age, income, and so forth. The following dissection was reported recently:[1]

- Naysayers—Consumers who are frightened and who have stopped buying optional goods altogether. They also started to seek out bargains related to their daily essential purchases and have switched to cheaper brands or even to cheaper stores. The members of this group are purported to be out of work, in danger of losing their jobs, or scared stiff that job loss might happen. They tend to have no savings cushion or limited savings only.
- Short-termers—Young urban consumers with little or no savings; they have lost nothing from the financial meltdown. They might even wonder what the fuss is all about and will carry on as normal. If they do lose their jobs, their consumption behavior has to change overnight. Suddenly they will have to find out what real essentials are.
- Long-termers—Older consumers who are concerned about their retirement savings but have seen downturns before, and they regard this crisis as a bad bump. They will adjust their consumption behavior to essentials and fewer impulse goods. They are looking primarily for value and foregoing some luxuries. They tend to be optimistic and are still consuming, but at a reduced rate.
- Simplifiers—Baby boomers who have lost a considerable amount of their savings and who have become risk averse and could be reassessing their values. Some might postpone retirement, and others might make do with less, reduce their consumption, and simplify their lives.

- Sympathizers—Consumers who were lucky or who had enough foresight to cash in before the real crash occurred. They spend at near normal levels, but do it discreetly because they do not want to be seen as flamboyant.
- Permabulls—Consumers who remain optimistic. For them, spending and shopping are part of life and are limited only by available credit. "Here today, gone tomorrow" is their motto.

Whether consumer segments such as this will stand the test of time and be useful beyond the current (2009) recession is up for debate. Also whether these somewhat vague but colorful segments are really useful is a moot point. In other words, can these segments really be identified and put to use for certain products, or will they remain strictly within the theoretical marketing sphere?

During a recession consumers will probably switch off when they hear or view advertisements based on fear appeals. There is enough bad news already! Advertising should rather concentrate on practical and value features of a product, emphasize trust in brand notions, and particularly stress comfort values, such as relationships, friendships and family. Recessions could also accelerate underlying trends such as online shopping and personal network building. Maybe marketers and advertisements can all help to get us from the "me only" to the "we together" society; who knows?

APPENDIX F

BEHAVIORAL ECONOMICS AND FINANCE

Economic and financial theory has always been based on the concept of *economic man*. Economic man makes logical and rational decisions, weighs the cost against benefits, balances the delay of current consumption against future consumption, and so forth. In short, economic man is a wonderful theoretical model for building economic theories. According to behavioral economics, this wonderful individual has only one shortcoming: namely, he does not exist.[1]

In real time, people tend to behave in an irrational, self-destructive, and even altruistic manner far removed from the logic associated with economic man on which economic theory was and still is based. Behavioral economics and her sister behavioral finance are the study of how real people actually make choices. They draw on insights from both economics and psychology, a fact that was recognized by Adam Smith as early as in 1759. Smith saw psychology as a part of decision making.[2]

In our modern society, people want instant gratification now, and they express the fervent desire to be much more patient in the future. Thus we tend to significantly devalue the future and concentrate on what we want now. For example, people say that they want to save for adverse conditions and retirement, eat healthier, start exercising, and quit smoking, and they mean it too, but not today. These virtues are firmly consigned to the future. Similarly, we buy things we can't afford on credit cards and as a result get to buy less over the course of our lifetimes, according to classical economics, anyway.

Proponents of behavioral economics note that traditional economic models often fail to predict outcomes in the real world. Behavioral insights can be used to enhance classical economic equations. Apparently these enhanced equations have predicted some outcomes correctly where more traditional methods have failed. But traditional economists are skeptical of the experimental and survey-based techniques used extensively in behavioral economics.

Behavioral finance tries to highlight inefficiencies, such as underreactions or overreactions to information and attribute them to limited investor attention, overconfidence and the herd instinct.[3] Also attention is paid to the lack of symmetry between decisions to acquire or keep resources—"the bird in the bush" paradox—and to the strong loss aversion or regret attached to any decision where some emotionally valued resources, such as shares or a physical asset such as a house, might be lost forever.[4]

Some of the foregoing discussion might help to explain our current *now* behavior at the expense of future consumption and supposedly long-term well-being. Whether all these additional theories and models have any significance for guiding us in the future to "smooth out" booms and busts remains to be seen. Nevertheless, the quest to explain our economic behavior and predict the future will always remain very interesting, but deceptively evasive at the same time. Probably just as well!

CHAPTER 1

1. "Greed and Fear," *Economist*, January 22, 2009: 3.

2. One of the most devastating of these was collateralized-debt obligations (CDOs). A CDO is a mechanism for converting mortgage securities and corporate bonds from huge, illiquid assets frequently owned by local investors into liquid financial instruments that could be traded across the world.

3. "Rebuilding the Banks," *Economist*, May 14, 2009: 1–3.

4. "Beware of Greeks Bearing Gilts," *Economist*, January 22, 2009: 1–3. Potential defaulters in the Euro Zone are referred to as PIGS: Portugal, Ireland, Greece, and Spain.

5. www.commongroundcommonsense.org/forums/index. php?showtopic=29894.

6. "A Hundred Factories Too Many," *Business Week*, January 12, 2009: 42–43.

7. "All You Need is Cash," *Economist*, November 20, 2008: 1–2

8. In "Going Overboard: Are Investment banks Run for Employees or Shareholders," in the *Economist*, July 16, 2009, the point is made that Goldman Sachs for the first half of 2009 allocated $4.4 billion in profit to shareholders and $11.4 billion in pay and bonuses. Also, an article by Andrew Clark in the *Guardian* newspaper in the United Kingdom entitled, "Is Goldman Sachs a Blood Sucking Vampire Squid?" did not beat about the bush. He asked the pertinent question whether we will keep allowing bankers to go back to enrich themselves through an elaborate, opaque form of casino trading, which is semidetached from the rest of society. (www.guardian. co.uk/business/andrew-clark-on-america/2009/jul/14/goldmansachs-banks).

9. Frank, R. H. and Cook, P. J., *The Winner-Take-All Society: Why the Few at the Top Get So Much More Than the Rest of Us*, Penguin Books, NY, USA, 1996.

10. In the past few years, close to 70% of business school graduates found employment in the financial services sector and consultancies at pretty high entrance salaries. With little or no practical general industry or life experiences and thus few real soft skills, these business graduates tended to be unemployable outside of these sectors. They were sometimes referred to as the "enthusiastic incompetents."

CHAPTER 2

1. An entrance barrier is the level to which new entrants to an industry need to commit financially in order to compete. For example, if you wanted to compete in the car manufacturing market, your entrance barrier would be very high, whereas competing in the Web shop market would require considerably less in financial resources. During the latter part of the boom period in Ireland (2004–2008) the saying was, "A pickup and a wheelbarrow, and Sean's your uncle, another building contractor."

2. As departmental managers for a very large multinational in the 1970s, my colleagues and I had to update the so-called doomsday scenario on a yearly basis.

3. The paradox of thrift was first labeled by the British Economist John Maynard Keynes (1883–1946).

4. Tulip mania or the tulip bulb bubble, was the first well-documented economic boom-bust cycle. This particular boom-bust dates back to 1647, when prices in Holland for tulip bulbs achieved astronomical levels due to investor speculation frenzies. The crash was just as dramatic. A nice account is given in *Tulipomania* by Mike Dash (2001).

5. A striking example: In 1970 Goldman Sachs had about 1300 employees. At the end of 2008, it had roughly 30,000. In 1971 Morgan Stanley had about 3,500 people; at the peak, in 2006, it had 55,000. (Quoted in, "How to Play Chicken and Lose," *Economist*, January 22, 2009:1–4.)

6. Fingleton, E., *In Praise of Hard Industries*, Orion Business, An imprint of the Orion Publishing Group Ltd., London, 1999.

7. See Appendix B: Some background to terms such as *knowledge economy* and *knowledge workers*.

8. "Career Ahead: Where will business students find work?" *Economist*, May 6, 2009: 1–2.

9. Some more thoughts on this are given in Appendix B.

10. *A Primer on the Knowledge Economy*, J. Houghton and P. Sheehan. Centre for Strategic Economic Studies, Victoria University, Melbourne, 2000: page 14.

11. "Bits and Atoms," N. Negroponte, *Wired* magazine, Wired Digital Inc, Issue 3.01, January 1995.

12. Fingleton, E., *In Praise of Hard Industries*, Orion Business, An imprint of the Orion Publishing Group Ltd., London, 1999.

13. In this respect it will be interesting to follow the UK economy from 2009 onward. This economy appears to have become overly reliant on so-called high-level services, financial services for one, and few real manufacturing industries remain.

14. "White Collars Turn Blue," Paul Krugman, published in the *New York Times* on September 29, 1996. (Note: This was written for a special centennial issue of *NYT Magazine*. The instructions were to write it as if it were in an issue 100 years in the future, looking back at the past century.)

15. See also Appendix B.

16. ICT; Information and Communication Technology.

17. Taylor, Kit Sims, "The Brief Reign of the Knowledge Worker: Information Technology and Technological Unemployment," paper presented at the international conference on the social impact of information technologies in St. Louis, Missouri, October 12–14, 1998.

18. Sims (1998).

19. www.nelh.nhs.uk/knowledge_management.

20. www.knowledgeboard.com/cgi_bin/item.cgi?id=119378.

21. This report can be found under, http://www.cecer.army.mil/kws/tho_lit.htm.

22. But who are we to judge? It reminds me of the expression describing a working environment as, "it's a madhouse here, and everyone thinks he is the only one on the staff."

23. Quoted from a Web site: http://blog.jackvinson.com/archives/2004/09/24/knowledge_worker_thread.html.

24. "Generation Y Goes to Work," the *Economist,* December 30, 2008, via www.economist.com.

25. Van Dijk (2008).

26. This always reminds me of a very popular British TV series from the seventies, *Yes Minister,* and later *Yes Prime Minister.* In one of the episodes, a senior civil servant asks his junior, "Are you a real high-flyer, or just a low-flyer supported by occasional gusts of wind?"

27. Frederick Winslow Taylor (1856–1915) is considered to be the father of scientific management.

28. Think of "the customer is central to our success," "we operate as an ethical organization well aware of our social responsibilities" and the all-time favorite, "we thrive because of our people."

CHAPTER 3

1. Frank, R. H. and Cook, P. J., *The Winner-Take-All Society: Why the Few at the Top Get So Much More Than the Rest of Us,* Penguin Books, NY, USA, 1996.

2. Van Dijk, T. J., "SME's and Globalisation: Opportunity, Threat or Both?" *Wits Business School Journal,* Johannesburg, January–March 2009; 52–54.

3. Chapter 2 under "In a Modern Knowledge Economy We Can Exist by Providing Services Only."

4. "Testing understanding": To check whether a previous statement made by someone else has been correctly understood by yourself. Most frequently used by experienced mediators in tough negotiation situations.

5. *Guerrilla Marketing: Secrets for Making Big Profits from Your Small Business.* Boston: Houghton Mifflin Company, 1984.

6. Belbin, M., *Management Teams: Why They Succeed or Fail,* Butterworth-Heinemann, 2003 (originally published in 1981).

7. In the context of his research; people with high mental ability and sharp analytical minds.

8. The term "Apollo Syndrome" has also been used to describe the condition in which someone has an exaggerated view of his or her role within a team. It is based on the anecdote that one person who claimed a critical role during the many 24–hour sessions for the Apollo Missions to the moon was the person who made the coffee to keep the scientists awake. Vital, perhaps, but critical?

9. Drucker, P. F., *Knowledge Work and Knowledge Society, The Social Transformation of this Century*, the 1994 Edwin L. Godwin Lecture at Harvard University, John F. Kennedy School of Government, May 4, 1994.

10. Belbin, M., *Management Teams: Why They Succeed or Fail*, Butterworth-Heinemann, 2003, (Originally published in 1981).

11. In the literature the term "Y Generation" is more commonly used, but I find the term "Net Geners" much more descriptive. After all, in the Human Resources jargon pot we already have theory Y, profile type Y, and no doubt other Y's to describe various phenomena.

12. "Managing the Face Bookers," *Economist,* December 30, 2008, via www.economist.com.

13. Such as "the search for meaning" or "the importance of the 'me' brand."

14. www.guardian.co.uk/money/2008/may/25/workandcareers.worklifebalance.

15. Not considered are companies that buy and sell other companies and judge them purely on financials. Conventional wisdom is that such a policy doesn't really make sense, except for the greater glory of management. Eventually most of these conglomerates break up once more.

16. It was reported recently (March 2009) that Japanese export sales, think car-makers, white goods, and so forth, had dropped by 40–50% since the latest (2008) recession started.

CHAPTER 4

1. See "Manage the Cash Flow and Your Bank," farther on in the chapter.

2. Under "team management skills" in Chapter 3.

3. A valuable lesson I learned from my own mentors in the '70s and '80s.

4. This in no way is meant as a derogatory remark. Certainly not for the many police and emergency services staffed by dedicated and committed professionals. The remark is made only to make a point to illustrate the ridiculous length some politicians, senior civil servants, and their consultants have gone to to "promote" the civil service. Let's just be kind and say it was another boom-time phenomenon that wasted taxpayer's money.

5. PACE, Product Awareness Call for Employees.

6. A large British bank that in 2008 wanted to introduce some unpopular measures for its "recent university graduate" overdrafts was faced with an online Facebook protest in which more than 4,000 students bad-mouthed the bank. The bank reversed its decision very quickly.

7. "Generation Y Goes to Work," *Economist*, December 30, 2008, via www.economist.com.

8. It's quite enlightening to share lunch facilities with all staff. It gets you down from the pedestal and sometimes even gives you some very useful insights if you are prepared to mingle properly and listen.

9. Unfortunately during a serious downturn, previously discussed innovative schemes, such as salary cuts, reduced hours, and forced vacations tend to be marginal in their effect and often prolong the agony of making the decision that is really required.

10. The latest trend (April 2009) to let banks in particular deviate from valuing assets not at the price a third party would pay, but rather at the price managers and regulators would like them to fetch is a lovely example of manipulating concepts to suit conditions. In other words; accounting standard bodies in the United States have been bullied into allowing bankers to exercise more judgment in how they grade and value illiquid assets.

11. This assumes that there is some demand and excess stock can be sold.

12. A simple but effective cash flow system is illustrated in *The Entrepreneur's Guide to Managing Growth and Handling Crises,* in Appendix C, written by the author and published by Praeger, Westport, CT, in 2008.

13. Private correspondence between the writer and Michael Hanley, CPA, Managing Partner of Merl & Hanley, LLP, Smithtown, NY.

14. If your company is a subscriber to a credit rating agency service you can monitor your company's credit rating as part of the service. If you feel that your credit rating is unjust, you might, presumably with pretty convincing supporting information provided on your behalf, get an adjustment to your rating.

15. There are a few other parameters that might influence this percentage, such as court injunctions and presumably your debt history, if a credit rating agency has been involved in your debt collections.

CHAPTER 5

1. See www.senicsme.com, under "You are not alone."

2. Second World War 1939–1945.

3. Correlations and standard deviations are statistical values that indicate the reliability of the measurements and the sample population.

4. *Financial Times,* April 8, 2009, and www.pricegrabber.com, consumer behavior report dated March 25, 2009.

5. "Chartists are Charlies" is an expression used extensively in business schools in the 1980s to belittle the study of stock markets and shares by examining historical trends and graphs and then projecting an identical pattern forward. A forecasting technique like that is based only on one premise—namely, that history repeats itself. It is particularly useless in volatile times and major industry upheavals. (So for that matter are all the sophisticated mathematical predictions that will fail just as miserably in turbulent times, as recently demonstrated!). Fortunately for all of us, the future remains unpredictable!

6. See also Van Dijk, T. J., *The Entrepreneur's Guide to Managing Growth and Handling Crises*, Praeger, Westport, CT, 2008.

7. The target consists of all the stakeholders, such as owners, employees, suppliers, etc.

8. Personally I have never considered conglomerates that take over any profitable company in any industry and add it to their portfolio as real takeover challenges. Acquisitions are judged purely on their financial performance. You are *in* when your return on investment (ROI) is acceptable; you're *out* when its not. Buying and selling of companies should be left to investors and the stock market, not to corporate management.

9. Collins, J. C., and Porras, J. I., *Built to Last: Successful Habits of Visionary Companies*. New York: Harper Business, 1994.

10. Van Dijk, T. J., *The Entrepreneur's Guide to Managing Growth and Handling Crises*. Praeger: Westport, CT, 2008.

11. "Time to put ideas into practice," *Economist* April 23, 2005 page 14. Also "Prime Cuts; Managing the Change," article in the *Irish Times*, April 6, 2009. (It quotes the Wharton Business School and PriceWaterHouseCoopers's report, "How to Build an Agile Foundation for Change.")

12. Apparently most individuals speak at the rate of 175 to 200 words per minute, but we are supposedly capable of listening and comprehending at 600 to 1,000 words a minute.

13. *SMS* stands for Short Message Service, a communication service standardized in the global system for mobile communication.

CHAPTER 6

1. Contrary to the "new economy" of the 1990s, economic developments that appear to have survived the initial hype and purely theoretical discussions are the concepts of behavioral economics and behavioral finance. A short description of these concepts is given in Appendix F.

2. Van Dijk, T. J., *The Entrepreneur's Guide to Managing Growth and Handling Crises*. Praeger: Westport, CT, 2008.

APPENDIX A

1. The original version of this tale was in German. It was given to me in 2002 by a management team member during an assignment in Germany. It was typed, on a real typewriter, you know (some of you might remember real typewriters), had obviously seen many readers, and had no credits or author given or even suggested. I asked whether I could copy it, and somehow this copy of the original German version survived many moves in my personal luggage. For the purposes of this book, I decided to translate the article into English. My translation follows

the imaginative idea only in a very general sense. Obviously, I neither would nor could lay claim to the original idea of this story, but can take credit only for my own rather free translation.

APPENDIX B

1. The six basic machines of classical antiquity are purported to have been the lever, the pulley, the screw, the balance, the wedge, and the wheel.

2. Prescriptive knowledge, together with propositional knowledge and tacit knowledge, forms the total knowledge set as defined by Mokyr (2002).

3. Sheehan, P. and Tegart, G. (Eds). *Working for the Future: Technology and Employment in the Global Knowledge Economy*, Victoria University Press, Melbourne, 1998.

4. Knowledge needs to be known. It always starts with individual information that is held in each human mind. Individual knowledge is of no use to a society as a whole unless it can be and is captured by external storage devices, such as books, drawings, presentations, manufactured articles, relics, etc. Mokyr (2002).

5. Drucker, P. F., "The next Society," *Economist*, November 1, 2001:1–4.

6. Drucker, P. F., "Knowledge Work and Knowledge Society, The Social Transformation of the Century," The 1994 Edwin L. Godwin Lecture at Harvard University, John F. Kennedy School of Government, May 4, 1994.

7. To me formal basic skills are reading, writing, and communication.

8. Reich, R. B., *The Work of Nations*, Vintage Books, New York, 1991.

9. Taylor, Kit Sims, "The Brief Reign of the Knowledge Worker: Information Technology and Technological Unemployment," paper presented at the International conference on the social impact of information technologies in St. Louis, Missouri, October 12–14, 1998.

10. Reference is made to private correspondence on this topic between Ken Wright of Wright Consultancy, Dublin, Ireland, and the writer.

11. An attempt in the 1970s to introduce employees as an asset in the balance sheet.

12. Davenport, T. H., Thomas R. J., and Cantrell, S., "The Mysterious Art and Science of Knowledge-Worker Performance," *MIT Sloan Management Review*, Fall 2002, Vol. 44, no. 1, 23–30.

13. Davenport, T. H., June 2003 (www.mywire/a/CIO/measurable-proposal/294552).

APPENDIX C

1. Krugman, P., "White Collars Turn Blue," *New York Times*, September 29, 1996.

2. Taylor, Kit Sims, "The Brief Reign of the Knowledge Worker: Information Technology and Technological Unemployment," paper presented at the International

conference on the social impact of information technologies in St. Louis, Missouri, October 12–14, 1998.

APPENDIX D

1. "SMEs and Globalisation: Opportunity, Threat or Both?" Theo J. van Dijk, *WBS Journal*, 52–54, January–March 2009.

2. *An Inquiry into the Nature and Causes of the Wealth of Nations*, written by Adam Smith in 1776.

3. *The Economist*, August 13, 2005, "From Mother Tongue to Meal Ticket."

4. During its long occupation of Ireland in the latter part of the twentieth century, a similar effort by the English occupiers to stamp out the use of Gaelic was equally ineffective.

5. It was reported in a Dutch newspaper, *De Telegraaf* of August 23, 2005, that Microsoft Windows XP would be available in the Frisian language. Frisian is a language in its own right that is spoken by fewer than a quarter of a million people in one of the Northern Provinces of The Netherlands called Friesland.

APPENDIX E

1. Quelch, J. A., Jocz, K. E., "Keeping a Keen Eye on Consumer Behaviour," *Financial Times*, February 5, 2009, special reports.

APPENDIX F

1. http://harvardmagazine.com/2006/03/the-marketplace-of-perce.html.

2. *The Theory of Moral Sentiments*, by Adam Smith, was published in 1759.

3. http://en.wikipedia.org/wiki/Behavioral_economics.

4. "A bird in the hand is worth two in the bush," a proverb meaning that it is better to go for certainty than for something speculative. The paradox is that investors will often not do a probability analysis for lowest risk/highest return. Rather, they will take their chances of getting something more speculatively rather than going for security.

BIBLIOGRAPHY

Belbin, M., *Management Teams—Why They Succeed or Fail*, Butterworth-Heinemann, 2003 (originally published in 1981).

Collins, J. C., and Porras, J. I., *Built to Last: Successful Habits of Visionary Companies.* New York: Harper Business, 1994.

Dash, M., *Tulipomania: The Story of the World's Most Coveted Flower and the Extraordinary Passion It Aroused,* Three Rivers Press, CA, 2001.

Davenport, T. H., Thomas, R. J. and Cantrell, S., "The Mysterious Art and Science of Knowledge-Worker Performance," *MIT Sloan Management Review,* Fall 2002, Vol. 44, no. 1, pages 23–30.

Drucker, P. F., "Knowledge Work and Knowledge Society, The Social Transformation of this Century," The 1994 Edwin L. Godwin Lecture at Harvard University, John F. Kennedy School of Government, May 4, 1994.

Drucker, P. F., "The Next Society," *Economist,* November 1, 2001: 1–4.

Fingleton, E., *In Praise of Hard Industries,* Orion Business, An imprint of the Orion Publishing Group Ltd., London, 1999.

Frank, R. H. and Cook, P. J., *The Winner-Take-All Society: Why the Few at the Top Get So Much More Than the Rest of Us,* Penguin Books, NY, 1996.

Houghton, J. and Sheehan, P., *A Primer on the Knowledge Economy,* Centre for Strategic Economic Studies, Victoria University, Melbourne, 2000.

Hylton, A. Dr., "Smaller Sized Companies Also Need Knowledge Management," www.eknowledgecenter.com/articles/1005/1005.htm, 2005.

Krugman, P., "White Collars Turn Blue," *NYT Magazine, New York Times*, September 29, 1996.

McCormack, M. H., *What They Don't Teach You at Harvard Business School,* Bantam Books, New York, 1986.

Mokyr, J., "The Knowledge Society: Theoretical and Historical Underpinnings," Presented to the Ad Hoc Expert Group on Knowledge Systems, United Nations New York, September 4–5, 2002.

Negroponte, N., "Bits and Atoms," *Wired* magazine, Issue 3.01, January 1995, Wired Digital Inc, USA. Also under www.wired.com.

Quelch, J. A. and Jocz, K. E., "Keeping a Keen Eye on Consumer Behaviour," *Financial Times* (UK), Special Report, February 5, 2009.

Reich, R. B., *The Work of Nations,* Vintage Books, New York, 1991.

Sheehan, P. and Tegart, G. (Eds.), *Working for the Future: Technology and Employment in the Global Knowledge Economy,* Victoria University Press, Melbourne, 1998.

Taylor, Kit Sims, "The Brief Reign of the Knowledge Worker: Information Technology and Technological Unemployment," paper presented at the International Conference on the Social Impact of Information Technologies in St. Louis, Missouri, October 12–14, 1998. Also under http:/online.bcc.ctc.edu/econ/kst/BriefReign/BRwebversion.htm.

Van Dijk, T. J., *The Entrepreneur's Guide to Managing Growth and Handling Crises,* Praeger, Westport, CT, USA, 2008.

Van Dijk, T. J., "SME's and Globalisation: Opportunity, Threat or Both?" *Wits Business School Journal,* Johannesburg, January–March 2009; 52–54.

INDEX

ABOUT THE AUTHOR

Theo J. van Dijk is an interim general manager for small to medium enterprises (SMEs) that encounter major difficulties. With twenty-plus years of experience in a variety of industries and countries, Theo has a hands-on, but above all, practical approach to getting SMEs back on track. As an internationally experienced turnaround and rescue manager, he has seen and worked in many difficult circumstances and tells it as it is. His style is first and foremost focused on practical management skills that make for a "lean and mean" approach in difficult times, but he also keeps a firm and "developing" eye on the future. He is the author of *The Entrepreneur's Guide to Managing Growth and Handling Crises,* a book in Praeger's Entrepreneur's Guide Series.